SOUTHERNMOST ART AND LITERARY PORTRAITS

Southernmost Art
and
Literary Portraits

FIFTY INTERNATIONALLY NOTED ARTISTS AND WRITERS IN THE SOUTH

Jimm Roberts

MERCER UNIVERSITY PRESS

2005

ISBN 0-86554-877-3
MUP/H697

Mercer University Press
1400 Coleman Avenue
Macon, Georgia 31207

First Edition.

Book design by Burt and Burt Studio

∞The paper used in this publication meets the minimum requirements
of American National Standard for Information Sciences—Permanence of Paper
for Printed Library Materials, ANSI Z39.48-1992.

Library of Congress Cataloging-in-Publication Data

Printed in Canada

FOR BARNEY AND LUCILLE

EDWARD ALBEE

RICHARD ANUSZKIEWICZ • ANN BEATTIE

JOHN MALCOLM BRINNIN • PHILIP BURTON • PHILIP CAPUTO

JOHN CHAMBERLAIN • JOHN CIARDI • HARRY CREWS • ANNIE DILLARD

MARJORY STONEMAN DOUGLAS • RICHARD EBERHART • DICK FRANCIS • MARILYN FRENCH

DUANE HANSON • JOHN HERSEY • CARL HIAASEN • EVAN HUNTER (ED McBAIN)

DONALD JUSTICE • WILLIAM KING • JAMES KIRKWOOD • JOHN KNOWLES

ELMORE LEONARD • ROY LICHTENSTEIN • ROBERT LUDLUM • ALISON LURIE

JOHN D. MacDONALD • THOMAS McGUANE • ROLLIE McKENNA • WILLIAM MANCHESTER

CONRAD MARCA-RELLI • JAMES MERRILL • JAMES A. MICHENER • JULES OLITSKI

LARRY POONS • PADGETT POWELL • ROBERT RAUSCHENBERG • LARRY RIVERS

JAMES ROSENQUIST • BOB SHACOCHIS • WILFRID SHEED • ISAAC B. SINGER

PATRICK D. SMITH • SYD SOLOMON • ROBERT STONE

PETER TAYLOR • JERRY N UELSMANN • RICHARD WILBUR

CHARLES WILLEFORD • JOY WILLIAMS

"We work in the dark—we do what we can—we give
what we have. Our doubt is our passion,
and our passion is our task. The rest is the madness of art."

Henry James

*H*ere are some microseconds of reality, some past moments sliced from the lives of fifty people—artists and authors—fixed forever in time and space by the lenses and imagination and vision of Jimm Roberts, photographer.

Some of these people are old and valued friends, some acquaintances, and all are, or were, respected contemporaries.

When I first agreed to write this introduction I had thought I would make a specific comment on particular photographs. But I realized at last that to do so would have led me into that gummy glade where reside the art critics muttering to each other about dynamic symmetry and mercurial impressionism. Of course they have yet to achieve the excesses of a literary critic falling upon what he or she has decided is a symbol.

So I will not try to interpret or describe. Jimm Roberts was concerned with expression, posture, the fall of the light, using these tiny slices of time to illuminate what he believed to be the essence of each person. He was using the outside to show us what seemed to him to be the inner climate of that creative person. It is a process of selection after many exposures have been taken. They were weeded down to a dozen or so. Oddly enough, many of that final group are the ones the photographer recognized at the moment the shutter clicked. He looked through the lens and a silent voice said, "That's it!" and he took the portrait. And finally there is the laboratory work, developing, printing, enlarging, exposure control—all styled to enhance that particular *something* which occasioned the excited "That's it!"

And this identical, indescribable *certainty* is what guides the hand and mind of the author and artist. In the middle of the long slow days and weeks comes that voice, "This is it!" Then comes the need for editing. Editing is the same in any medium, undertaken for the same purpose: to capture more clearly, to refine, to enhance. And we all labor under an identical burden, an unsteady grasp upon objectivity. Is this what I think it is? Have I done my best with it? Was the voice wrong when it spoke to me? In the end, the work of art, be it in print or paint or silver bromide, must stand by itself and be examined by the world.

Jimm Roberts added a subtle dimension to this presentation by dealing with people who work or have worked in Florida. Hernando DeSoto described it to his King as a sand pit unfit for human habitation. Despite many recent improvements designed to prove DeSoto was right, it has served as a useful habitation for work and play for a great many writers and artists.

People totally involved in life-long creative effort are subjected to a certain amount of curiosity. This can be irritating and frustrating in a small town environment. A person of a mild degree of eccentricity can become the town hobby. Creative work is difficult in a big city. Nobody cares about one's lifestyle or work habits, but the anthill hubbub is stressful and, in time, enervating. And so one goes to small towns and small cities in resort areas for a combination of those two worlds. One has the freedom of the big city, and the selective silence of a small town. So it is no mystery why creative people settle in Taos and Cannes and Santa Barbara and Sarasota.

And that is what gives these photographic studies a special flavor. Jimm Roberts has taken pains to depict all of us in our chosen environment. You will notice that there is, in some odd way, a persistent flavor of isolation, privacy, almost secretiveness. And that is as it should be. All of these people prefer to be known through their work. It is their true identity. Jimm Roberts has tried, with remarkable success, to give clues to the other identity, the hidden one, the face behind the face, the one that watches the world and turns it into his or her own vision.

John D. MacDonald
Siesta Key, 1986

"Photography is important because it takes a moment and makes it an eternity, and so goes art, if it's right."

❦

Isaac Bashevis Singer

*I*ndividuals who have sat for Jimm Roberts—especially those who have done so more than once—discover that he shares a professional secret with the most illustrious of his colleagues who deal in portraiture. This is his way of giving subjects the time to put on a best "face"—to make what they consider the best presentation or projection of themselves—even as he takes his own good time to arrive at assessments often quite at variance with theirs. In spite of a scrupulous regard for the feelings of his subjects, Roberts often finds them looking less at the camera than at the cameraman. "I'm all here," says the subject. "What is that young man going to *do* with me?" What "that young man" does is to photograph the question, so to speak, then answer it with a decisive portrait that makes the operations of the ego irrelevant.

Respecting the tendency of subjects to choose their own settings and surround themselves with their own icons, Roberts finds that these efforts do not always produce the effects intended. Self-placement can lead to self-caricature or cloying cuteness; it can also lead subjects to moments when their self-consciousness is relaxed and they betray their own intentions—like a child who, offering a doll to the camera, is unaware that the photographer has found just that moment of character study which the absence of the doll would have delayed or obscured.

Most of the writers and painters depicted here are shown in close relation to the tools of their trades. Much like the guildsmens' leather aprons, their anvils, mortars, alembics, and balanced pans, these accoutrements, after all, are what define subjects as persons of accomplishment and provide them with professional security at the moment of their "exposure." A writer or a painter caught sniffing a rose is anonymous. But one with a half-written page in the Smith Corona or one who stands beside a painting barely dry means business that does not have to be explained.

Six or seven years ago, I became one of Jimm Roberts' willing subjects. At the time, I felt no compulsion to tell him that I had traveled and worked for months on end with the great Cartier-Bresson and, as well, with Rollie McKenna, one of the most eminent of American photographers whose particular focus has been on artists in their lairs. Nor did I mention that circumstance had allowed me many opportunities to discuss photography—both as fieldwork and as an exercise in metaphysics—with the legendary Man Ray ("Every portrait I've ever made has been taken upside down"), and with other masters such as Walker Evans, Robert Frank, Edward Weston and the late Thomas Victor. Jimm eventually came to know of these illuminating encounters and, undaunted, has entrusted me to say what I've observed of his own professional stance and outlook in the years between.

First, I've been aware of constants that dictate his method; then of changes in technique that reflect both refinement and expansion of his original premises. These constants might best be categorized as temperamental: respect for his subjects sometimes verging on adulation, a modesty so disarming that anyone sitting for him wants to make the occasion a cooperative venture, a kind of pragmatic innocence that leads him to believe what he sees and thus avoid the demeaning excesses of the candid as carefully as he eschews the studio-appointment banalities of the posed. As for technique—if, finally, it is indeed something separable from an attitude—Jimm's is based upon the resourceful use of a good camera in the services of a patiently discerning eye. He does not stalk his subjects, but waits upon them, alert to every shift in mood or alteration of setting that might reveal another facet of character or an unexpected, sometimes whimsical, conjunction of person and place.

Person and place—in one way or another, the artists in this collection, native or adoptive, are Floridians. Indifferent to pictorial cliches that might stress the fact, Jimm, by accident or design, has subtly conveyed a sense of what it's like to live in Florida and made that a leitmotif running through exhibition space and across these pages. The hats are of straw; the clothing summery and informal; the decor spare and transiently makeshift. Windows are bright and, shaded or not, each opens onto this or that species of native flora crowding the sills.

Portable—a traveling exhibit, a book in the hand—this gallery of portraits is nonetheless permanent. Not too many years from now, historians of art and chroniclers of literary taste will investigate the surprisingly swift growth of Florida as a state of mind and climate congenial to American artists of the most diverse persuasions. They will develop intriguing theories; attempt to fit Siesta Key and Key West into one lumpy Procrustean bed with Miami Beach and Sarasota; and put forth speculations—about artists who sought roots, those who seemed bent on escape, those who simply needed haven. By that time, most of their theories will have been disproved, their speculations dismissed. But chances are that at least some of these cultural anthropologists will have retained enough of simple human curiosity to ask, "Who were these artists? What did they look like?" Thanks to Jimm Roberts' energy and discrimination—not to mention the range of a lens that misses no contour of a particular human landscape—the answers they will seek in retrospect can be found right here.

John Malcolm Brinnin
Key West, 1994

SOUTHERNMOST ART AND LITERARY PORTRAITS

THE PORTRAITS

EDWARD ALBEE

"I've always thought that a person is pretty much what he turns out to be from the very beginning. You just have to find out who you are. I am a playwright: that's one of the people I am. I resisted it for a very long time, although I did write a play when I was about twelve which my mother threw away—wise woman. I made a couple of dreadful half-assed beginnings of plays in my twenties. I wrote novels, poetry, and short stories from the age of about eight to twenty-eight and they weren't any good either. Then when I was twenty-nine I wrote *The Zoo Story*, and my whole life changed."

EDWARD ALBEE was born on March 12, 1928, in Washington, DC. He has been acclaimed as one of America's foremost playwrights since the first production (October 13, 1962) of *Who's Afraid of Virginia Woolf?*, a play that received the New York Drama Critics Circle Award, two Tony Awards, and the Foreign Press Association Award, among others in 1963. Other early plays by Albee include: *The Zoo Story* (1958), *The Death of Bessie Smith* (1959), *The Sandbox* (1959), and *The American Dream* (1960). His later plays, *A Delicate Balance* (1966), *Seascape* (1975), and *Three Tall Women* (1994), won Pulitzer Prizes. Albee is a member of the American Academy of Arts and Letters. He lives in New York City, Montauk, Long Island, as well as Coconut Grove, Florida.

COCONUT GROVE, 1990

RICHARD ANUSZKIEWICZ

"The image of my work has always been determined by what I wanted the color to do. Color function becomes my subject matter and its performance is my painting."

RICHARD ANUSZKIEWICZ was born May 23, 1930, in Erie, Pennsylvania. His paintings present a formal approach to the interplay of color that set off the 1960s movement Optical Art. In viewing a canvas by Anuszkiewicz, the observer will experience spatial distortion and, at times, dizzying vibrations of color. By utilizing the interaction of contrasting colors of full intensity, Anuszkiewicz explores the potential effects of optical mix. He lives in Englewood, New Jersey, and Sarasota, Florida.

MELBOURNE, 1986

ANN BEATTIE

"I thought about writing seriously, as opposed to thinking about writing as a career, when I started graduate school in the early '70s. I had always been a big reader and I'm an only child and my parents read a lot to me. As a little kid I wrote stories. In high school I wrote some bad poetry. When I got to undergraduate school I learned that you had to read very carefully.

I was certainly not particularly gifted at writing and it's not as though I did it exclusively. I thought that the world was open with possibilities in those days. There were many things I was trying to be—a hippie among them. Writing was a nighttime activity; it was sort of my hobby. I didn't think about it in even remotely practical terms. I just thought that I wanted to do more of this to see if I could get better at it and, if I were to do this, I would need to learn some things."

ANN BEATTIE was born September 8, 1947, in Washington, DC. Often cited as "the voice of her generation," she is the widely acclaimed author of the novels: *Chilly Scenes of Winter, Falling in Place, Love Always, Picturing Will, My Life, Starring Dara Falcon,* and *The Doctor's House.* Her short story collections include *Distortions, Secrets and Surprises, The Burning House, Where You'll Find Me, What Was Mine, Park City, Perfect Recall,* and *Follies: New Stories.* Other works include *Alex Katz* (art criticism), and *Spectacles* (a book for children). Her stories have appeared in four O'Henry Award collections, John Updike's *Best American Short Stories of the Century,* and in magazines such as the *New Yorker, Esquire, G.Q.,* and *Virginia Quarterly Review.* In 1978 she received a Guggenheim Fellowship, and in 2000 the Pen/Malamud Award for excellence in short fiction. Ann Beattie is a member of the American Academy of Arts and Letters. She divides her time between Charlottesville, Virginia; York, Maine; and Key West, Florida.

KEY WEST, 1997

John Malcolm Brinnin

"Most of us became writers because we were obsessive readers. Except for the twenty volumes of *The Book of Knowledge*, children's literature—even Tom Swift, the Bobbsey Twins and the ragged overachievers of Horatio Alger—left me cold.

Finding my indiscriminate way to Proust and Joyce, Whitman, Hart Crane and Gertrude Stein by the time I was twelve, I simply tore through *A Child's Garden of Verse* and leapt a hedge into adulthood. But not without moments of penance: my one book for children—about a dolphin named Arthur—has just been reissued in France, with illustrations by the great Andre Francois.

For me, becoming a writer was never a decision but a development recognized too late for reconsideration. The 'decision' aside, I see my turning to writing as but another attempt of the ego to get through the looking glass and discover what's left."

JOHN MALCOLM BRINNIN was born September 13, 1916, in Halifax, Nova Scotia. He was a poet, critic, biographer, social historian, and chronicler of the literary scene from the era of Gertrude Stein's Parisian salon to the late 1900's. Brinnin was the director of the historic YM-YWHA Poetry Center in New York and was a member of the American Academy of Arts and Letters. His books include six volumes of poetry; the non-fiction classic, *Dylan Thomas in America*, as well as *The Third Rose: Gertrude Stein and Her World*, *Sextet*, *Truman Capote: Dear Heart, Old Buddy*, which *Newsweek* called "an exemplary piece of work," and *The Sway of the Grand Saloon: A Social History of the North Atlantic*. John Malcolm Brinnin lived in Key West, Florida. He died June 25, 1998.

KEY WEST, 1985

Philip Burton

"I grew up in a mining village in South Wales that was theatre-struck. As a young boy I saw Shakespeare there, I saw opera there, I saw Gilbert and Sullivan there. It was amazing! Then, when I started to read, Shakespeare became the love of my life. I've never lost that love or the desire to learn more about him. I've written two books about him—the first public lecture I ever gave in America was "The Miracle That Was Shakespeare," because it is remarkable what he achieved with what he began with."

PHILIP BURTON was born November 30, 1904, in Mountain Ash, Wales. He was a Shakespearean scholar, actor, writer, director and Richard Burton's mentor. His non-fiction books include *Early Doors: My Life and the Theatre*, *The Sole Voice: Character Portraits from Shakespeare*, a Shakespeare novel *You, My Brother*, and the children's book *The Green Isle*. Philip Burton lived in Key West, Florida. He died January 28, 1995.

KEY WEST, 1988

PHILIP CAPUTO

"One does not decide to become a writer in the sense that one decides to become a lawyer, doctor, or stock broker. The writing of serious literature is not a means to earn a living. Neither is it a profession. It is a motivation in the original meaning of the word; that is, a calling. It is also a way of life. Thus, the decision is made for him, not by him. To be sure, there were influences and events in my life that nudged me in a literary direction, but I think I was destined, for better or worse, to do this from the moment I was born."

PHILIP CAPUTO was born June 10, 1941, in Chicago, Illinois. He is the widely acclaimed author of *A Rumor of War*, which was produced as a film. His other books include *Horn of Africa, DelCorso's Gallery, Indian Country, Equation for Evil, Exiles* (a book consisting of three short novels), and *The Voyage*. As a reporter for the *Chicago Tribune* in 1972, he shared the Pulitzer Prize for investigative reporting with three other reporters. Caputo went on to serve as a correspondent for the *Chicago Tribune* in Rome, Moscow, Beirut, and won the Overseas Press Club's George Polk Citation in 1973. His 1991 memoir, *Means of Escape*, recounts his years and adventures as a foreign correspondent. Set principally in the 1990's, his 2005 novel *Acts of Faith*, draws upon Caputo's first hand knowledge of war and first hand reportorial experience to give a powerful unblinking account of the "goings-on" at the height of Sudan's civil war. A resident of Key West from 1977 until about 1986, he now lives in Norwalk, Connecticut.

KEY WEST, 1983

JOHN CHAMBERLAIN

"Franz Shubert was my first hero. If I hadn't discovered Franz Shubert when I was twelve I probably would have ended up being a dumb aeronautical engineer somewhere. I was really into airplanes before I was twelve. If I had stayed into airplanes I probably would have gone to Purdue and gotten a real job. But then I discovered Franz Shubert. Every time I listen to the 'Unfinished' Symphony no. 8 in B Minor, I break down and cry—he's marvelous. Now I'm a late, first-edition abstract expressionist."

JOHN CHAMBERLAIN was born April 16, 1927, in Rochester, Indiana. His best known works are the baroque, abstract sculptures he creates from the exterior panels of junk cars, which he assembles, squeezes, and compresses, making use of pre-existing and applied colors in his unique compositions. In 1993, he received the Lifetime Achievement Award from the International Sculpture Center in Washington, DC. He is a member of the American Academy of Arts and Letters. A resident of Sarasota, Florida from 1980 to 1990, John Chamberlain now lives on Shelter Island, New York.

SARASOTA, 1983

JOHN CIARDI

"As a young boy I was an avid and indiscriminate reader. I had stacks of tattered dime novels; Horatio Algers, Tom Swifts, Rover Boys, and a one-volume encyclopedia, a gift from my mother which I read until the pages came apart.

In college, at Tufts, which was nearly in my backyard, I found John Holmes. He was the first published poet I had ever known. I signed up for his writing course and almost at once, I knew what I was going to do with the rest of my life. I had no idea how I would get by, but I was ready to go for broke."

JOHN CIARDI was born June 24, 1916, in Boston, Massachusetts. A prolific writer, translator, and literary critic, his books of poems include *Homeward to America* (1940), *A Sheaf of Love Poems* (1958), and *Fast and Slow Poems for Advanced Children and Beginning Parents* (1975). He received the Oscar Blumenthal Prize for Poetry in 1943, the Eunice Tietjens Memorial Prize for Poetry in 1944, the Levinson Prize for Poetry in 1946, and the Rome Fellowship for Literature from the American Academy of Arts and Letters in 1956. Ciardi hosted the CBS TV show *Accent* and was poetry editor for *Saturday Review* from 1977 to 1979. His translation of Dante's *Divine Comedy* is considered the definitive translation and his fascination with words and language led to the etymological volumes, *The Browser's Dictionary and Native's Guide to the Unknown American Language*. A member of the American Academy of Arts and Letters, John Ciardi lived in Metuchen, New Jersey and Key West, Florida. He died April 1, 1986.

KEY WEST, 1985

HARRY CREWS

"I can't remember when I first decided to become a writer because I can't remember when I did not want to be a writer. That came part and parcel with my life. I didn't understand it in terms of being a writer, but as soon as I found out there was such a thing as a writer—I wanted to be one. I wanted to tell stories. I've never successfully found the beginning of that nor the trigger that brought it about. In the *Childhood* book I say, 'I've come up from a society of storytelling people.'

I rather agree with Thomas Wolfe when he said, 'We are the sum of all our moments.' I think that everything that ever happened to me, in one way or another, influenced me, in one direction or another."

HARRY CREWS was born June 6, 1935, in Alma, Georgia. One of the more remarkable and original storytellers of his generation, he has written over two dozen acclaimed books including the novels *The Gospel Singer*, *A Feast of Snakes*, *The Gypsy's Curse*, *Karate Is a Thing of the Spirit*, *Car*, *All We Need of Hell*, *Body*, *The Mulching of America*, and *Celebration*. Among his non-fiction works are two collections of essays: *Blood and Grits*, and *Florida Frenzy*, as well as his widely praised memoir, *A Childhood: The Biography of a Place*, which was critically hailed as a literary masterpiece. Crews's play, *Blood Issue*, was produced by the Actors Theater of Louisville in 1989. He received an Award in Literature from the American Academy of Arts and Letters in 1972 and a National Endowment for the Arts Award in 1974. Additional stories and essays by Crews have appeared in *Esquire*, *Harper's* and *Playboy*. He lives in Gainesville, Florida.

GAINESVILLE, 1983

ANNIE DILLARD

"I was always going to be a painter, although I studied literature in college. Then after college, I thought I really should do something about this interest in painting I had going. I was painting a still life, standing there working at the easel morning, noon, and night. One day it occurred to me—I could be sitting down. So I went back to writing.

Writing is such a crazy thing to be doing with your days—ruining little pieces of paper. It's nice to have other people around who consider that a reasonable thing to do all day. In fact, there's a group of writers here in Key West that are also some of the best writers there are—Robert Stone, Joy Williams, Ann Beattie, Richard Wilbur, Phyllis Rose, and Alison Lurie.

Once I'm well under way on a work, I can work anywhere. I always set up my study so that I'm looking at a blank wall—except for here."

ANNIE DILLARD was born April 30, 1945, in Pittsburgh, Pennsylvania. In 1975, she received the Pulitzer Prize for *Pilgrim at Tinker Creek*. The *New Republic* noted, "There is no way to avoid seeing again after you have read Annie Dillard." Her other non-fiction books include *An American Childhood*, *Teaching a Stone to Talk*, *Living by Fiction*, *The Writing Life*, *Holy the Firm*, and *For the Time Being*. She has written two books of poetry: *Tickets for a Prayer Wheel*, and *Mornings Like This: Found Poems*. Dillard's first novel, *The Living*—about four men on the Pacific Northwest frontier—was published in 1992. Annie Dillard is founder of the Saturday Morning Beach Volleyball, Key West, and a member of the American Academy of Arts and Letters. She divides her time between Middletown, Connecticut; Cape Cod, Massachusetts; and Key West, Florida.

KEY WEST, 1993

MARJORIE STONEMAN DOUGLAS

"I did not think about being a writer. All I wanted to do was to write. I never wanted to do anything else in my life. I first saw my own writing in print when I was ten years old. It was a short piece for the children's section of a Boston newspaper. I never forgot the thrill. I began to write continuously at fourteen for my high school paper which came out monthly. It was the Taunton, Massachusetts, high school paper called *The Stylus*. When I went to college in 1908, from which I graduated in 1912, I majored in English composition and was printed in the Wellsley magazine very often."

MARJORIE STONEMAN DOUGLAS was born April 7, 1890, in Minneapolis, Minnesota. She was an active environmentalist in saving the Florida Everglades. Her literary contributions include The *Everglades: River of Grass*, *Hurricane*, *Freedom River*, *Alligator Crossing*, *Florida: The Long Frontier*, and her autobiography, *Voice of the River*, written with John Rothchild. In 1993, President Clinton presented her with the Medal of Freedom, the country's highest civilian award. Marjorie Stoneman Douglas lived in Coconut Grove, Florida. She died May 14, 1998, at the age of 108.

COCONUT GROVE, 1986

Richard Eberhart

"When I was about fifteen or sixteen years old in Austin, Minnesota, I started reading Tennyson and fell in love with his work entirely—because of the beauty of the language, and the mellifluous quality of his lines, and the marvelous perfect rhymes. It never occurred to me until I got to be about sixty years old, and I haven't mentioned this before, but I think I owe the beginning of my poetry to Alfred Lord Tennyson."

RICHARD EBERHART was born April 5, 1904, in Austin, Minnesota. He remains one of America's most honored senior poets. In 1962 he received the Bollingen Prize, in 1966 the Pulitzer Prize for *Selected Poems 1930–1965*, and the National Book Award in 1977 for *Collected Poems 1930–1976*. In April 1986 he was awarded the Robert Frost Medal from the Poetry Society of America. Among his other works are *The Quarry*, *Fields of Grace*, *Survivors*, and *Ways of Sight*. A member of the American Academy of Arts and Letters, he served as Poet Laureate on the United States from 1959–1961. Richard Eberhart lived in Gainesville, Florida and Hanover, New Hampshire. He died June 14, 2005 at the age of 101.

GAINESVILLE, 1989

DICK FRANCIS

"I was riding the Queen Mother's horse Devon Loch in the 1956 Grand National in England. I was 10 lengths in front, 25 yards from the winning post, and the horse collapsed with me. I've looked at the newsreel film many times. It's never been satisfactorily decided what did actually happen. My author's agent thought that was a peg on which to hang an autobiography. I had been champion jockey and Queen Mother's jockey and he thought I had a story to tell.

The *Sport of Queens* was published in December 1957. My first novel *Dead Cert* was published in the spring of 1962 and there's been one every year ever since."

DICK FRANCIS was born October 31, 1920, in Tenby, Wales. He was the Queen Mother's jockey and Britain's Grand National Champion rider. Now a best-selling mystery writer, his intrigues are set against horse racing backgrounds. Francis has written over thirty-five books which include the blockbusters *Break In*, *Bolt*, *Hot Money*, *Blood Sport*, *High Stakes*, *Rat Race*, and *Banker*. He received the Edgar Allan Poe Award for *Forfeit* in 1969, for *Whip Hand* in 1980, for *Come to Grief* in 1996, as well as a Grand Master award for his lifetime achievement, also in 1996—all from the Mystery Writers of America. In addition, Francis was the recipient of the Crime Writers' Association's rarely bestowed accolade, the Cartier Diamond Dagger Award in 1989. A resident of Ft. Lauderdale from 1983 until 1993, he now lives on Grand Cayman Island in the Caribbean.

FT. LAUDERDALE, 1988

Marilyn French

"Well, my mother tells me that when I had to write my first composition in the fourth grade on "What do you want to be when you grow up?" I said I wanted to be a book writer. I don't remember this. I do remember a period from about the ages of eight to twelve when I decided I would be a composer, until it dawned on me women weren't allowed to do that. There was only one woman composer I knew about and that was Cecile Chaminade, and she had obviously not been major. So I gave that up and went back to intending to be a writer. There wasn't anytime in my conscious life when I didn't want to write.

I worked for twenty years before *The Women's Room* was published and the style of that is very carefully calculated to express a particular world view. The narrator of the book is not superior to the actors in it. She's not superior to the reader. She's someone you could be listening to across a kitchen table, drinking coffee. She is stumbling her way through experience just as the reader is stumbling the way through their experience. Her rage is palpable—as women's rage is palpable across kitchen tables—and so is the poignancy of her situation…"

MARILYN FRENCH was born Mara Solwaska, November 21, 1929, in New York City. She is the author of the bestselling novels *The Women's Room*, *The Bleeding Heart*, and *Her Mother's Daughter*; two works of literary criticism, *The Book as World: James Joyce's Ulysses* and *Shakespeare's Division of Experience*; and two works of social criticism, *Beyond Power: Women, Men, And Morals* and *The War Against Women*. She lives in New York City and on Singer Island, Florida.

SINGER ISLAND, 1992

DUANE HANSON

"Carl Milles, the great Swedish sculptor who worked under Rodin, once said to me when I was a student in Cranbrook Academy of Art, 'Do good work and you will be recognized.' I thought he was simple-minded for saying that. But on June 3, 1986, I had a number of sculptures in his old studio in Stockholm. King Carl XVI Gustaf came to the opening and shook my hand.

Being an artist was never a decision. I had always been self-motivated and made paintings and sculptures as a child without any outside motivation or instruction. At present, I'm very interested in translating my approach of illusionist sculpture into bronze for the sake of durability and the opportunity for doing work which can exist outside."

DUANE HANSON was born January 17, 1925, in Alexandria, Minnesota. The artist is seen here with the figure of a young girl that, in fact, is a sculptural rendering of his daughter. By utilizing everyday subjects, the super-realistic sculptor causes the viewer to focus on people who are unsmiling, that appear lonely and often passed by in life. From his live subject, he makes a mould which is cast in polyester resin, then meticulously painted. They are technical masterpieces in every detail, even to the utilization of clothing and human hair. Duane Hanson lived in Davie, Florida. He died January 6, 1996.

DAVIE, 1983

JOHN HERSEY

"I think I've always wanted to write. I tried to write a biography of President Wilson when I was ten years old. I'm afraid I only got one or two sentences down on paper, but the impulse was there. It came from having read I'm sure."

JOHN HERSEY was born June 17, 1914, in Tientsin, China. His first postgraduate job, in the summer of 1937, was as private secretary to Sinclair Lewis. Following his service to Lewis he worked as a journalist and war correspondent for *Time*. After the war, Hersey signed on as a correspondent and editor for *Life* and *The New Yorker*. His first novel, *A Bell for Adano*, won the Pulitzer Prize in 1945 and was produced as a film. Since 1947, he devoted most of his time to writing fiction. Hersey's ten books of reportage and essays and fifteen works of fiction include *Hiroshima, The Wall, A Single Pebble, The War Lover, The Algiers Motel Incident, Aspects of the Presidency, Blues, Antonietta*, and two collections of stories, *Fling*, and *Key West Tales*. He was chancellor of the American Academy of Arts and Letters 1981–1984. John Hersey lived in Vineyard Haven, Massachusetts, and Key West, Florida. He died March 24, 1993.

KEY WEST, 1989

CARL HIAASEN

"I had a very middle-class uneventful childhood. I didn't have the kind of experiences Jack London had and I wasn't going to go out and be able to write those kind of books. But there was one way to get a dose of reality and learn about people—learn how people talk, learn to listen, to take notes, to observe. Nothing trains you better for that than journalism and working on newspapers. A newspaper enforces the discipline of writing. You're on a deadline and you cannot afford to get writer's block. I think that's why a lot of writers come out of a journalism background.

When you're starting it's a hell of a way to learn about the world. It makes the work of writing books a little easier because you know you can string a couple of sentences together and have them make sense."

CARL HIAASEN was born March 12, 1953, in Fort Lauderdale, Florida. He is an award-winning columnist and reporter for the *Miami Herald*, where he has worked since 1976. His vastly popular novels, which together have been translated into twenty-two languages, include *Tourist Season*, *Double Whammy*, *Skin Tight*, *Native Tongue*, *Strip Tease* (which was made into a film), *Stormy Weather*, *Basket Case*, *Lucky You*, *Sick Puppy*, and *Skinny Dip*. Hiaasen has also contributed lyrics to two songs by Warren Zevon: "Seminole Bingo" and "Rottweiler Blues." He lives in the Florida Keys.

PLANTATION, 1990

Evan Hunter (Ed McBain)

"I made the decision to become a writer while I was in the US Navy during World War II. Up to that time, I was studying art. I simply decided I was a better writer than I was a painter. I've never experienced a so-called 'dry spell.' I write from nine in the morning to five in the evening, five days a week, and I write about the same number of words each year."

EVAN HUNTER was born October 15, 1926, in New York City. He is a prolific writer whose novels include *The Blackboard Jungle*, *Strangers When We Meet*, and *The Streets of Gold*. He also writes the 87th Precinct mystery series under the pseudonym Ed McBain. His screenplays include Alfred Hitchcock's *The Birds* and *Strangers When We Meet*. Hunter received the Edgar Allen Poe Award in 1957, the coveted Grand Master Award from the Mystery Writers of America in 1986, and in 1998 he was the first American to receive a Carter Diamond Dagger from the Crime Writers Association of Great Britain. Evan Hunter lived in Weston, Connecticut and Siesta Key, Florida. He died July, 6, 2005.

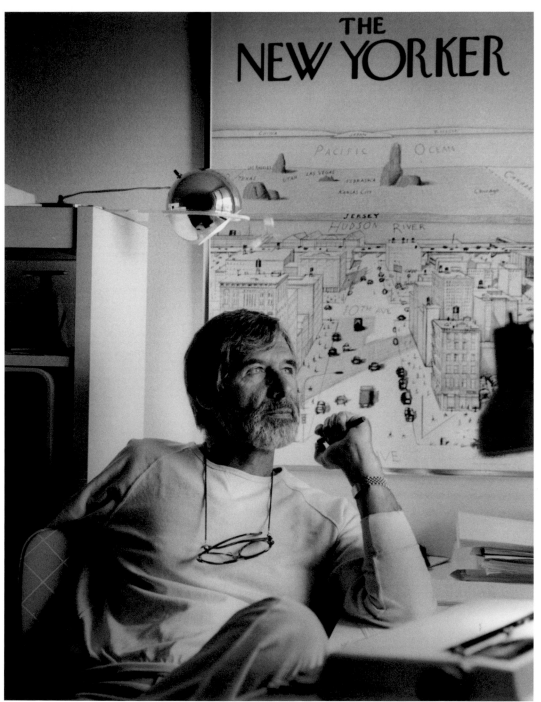

SIESTA KEY, 1983

DONALD JUSTICE

"The decision to write must have come in late adolescence or the early years of college. What provoked it, I think, was the realization that I would never be able to write music the way I had wanted to. Eventually it turned out that I liked writing poetry and seemed to be better at doing it. That's how I settled in as a poet."

DONALD JUSTICE was born August 12, 1925, in Miami, Florida. Acclaimed for his formalist verse, as well as his teaching skills, he won the Pulitzer Prize in 1980 for *Selected Poems* and the Bollingen Award in 1991. His other books of poetry include *The Sunset Maker*, *Night Light*, *Departures*, and *Collected Poems*. Justice received grants in poetry from the Rockefeller Foundation, the Guggenheim Foundation, and the National Council on the Arts, and in theater from the Ford Foundation. A member of the American Academy of Arts and Letters, he was a resident of Gainesville, Florida, from 1982 until 1992. Justice then moved to Iowa City, Iowa. He died August 6, 2004.

GAINESVILLE, 1988

WILLIAM KING

"I left Florida with an older woman when I was twenty in June, 1945. My mother gave me a hundred bucks and said, 'You better get out of this state—there's nothing here for anybody between the ages of sixteen and seventy-five.' I got to New York two days after the airplane flew into the Empire State Building. I thought, "*What* a town!"

I always was an artist, but I didn't know it. I decided to become a sculptor in New York City on October 28, 1945. That was the date of an exhibition of David Smith's sculpture at 32 East 57th Street. Our drawing teacher, Sidney Delavante at Cooper Union, took us to see it."

WILLIAM KING was born on January 25, 1925, in Jacksonville, Florida. His sculptural forms, inventive figures that display commonplace gestures, cause the viewer to feel as if they are seeing this gesture for the first time—as if they are rediscovering something familiar. Utilizing materials from vinyl to stainless steel, producing figures measured in inches to those several times life size, King's sculpture often conveys a sense of joy and well-being. William King lives in East Hampton, New York, and Coral Gables, Florida.

CORAL GABLES, 1988

JAMES KIRKWOOD

"I had always been an actor, from age fourteen to my late twenties, but after a TV soap I'd been on for four years went off the air, I moved back to the place of my birth, Southern California. Went for a long time without work—it was like getting started all over again. Finally woke up in the middle of the night, sweating, thinking I must find something I can do everyday by myself, can't just sit around waiting for acting jobs to materialize, for the phone to ring. I set up an office at two in the morning and decided to write a novel based on the body of my mother's fiancée which I'd found in our backyard (a suicide) when I was fourteen. Although I'd never written anything before, I just slammed away. And when I finished—it was published. *There Must Be A Pony!*—first novel."

JAMES KIRKWOOD was born August 22, 1930, in Los Angeles, California. Playwright and author, his best-known work is the highly acclaimed musical *A Chorus Line*. Kirkwood received the Pulitzer Prize in Drama (1976), the Tony Award (1976), the Drama Desk Award, the Drama Critics Circle Award, and the Theater World Award, all for *A Chorus Line*. He is also the author of the play *There Must Be A Pony* and the screenplay *Some Kind of Hero*, both based on his novels of the same titles. Following the production of his most recent play, *Legends* (with Mary Martin and Carol Channing), he wrote his memoir, *Diary of a Mad Playwright*, published in 1989. James Kirkwood lived in New York City and East Hampton, New York; and Key West, Florida. He died April 21, 1989.

KEY WEST, 1988

JOHN KNOWLES

"My father read the popular magazine of that period for so-called middle-brow Americans—*The Saturday Evening Post*. I started to read it and thought I could write better stories than these. I was twelve at the time.

Then when I was nineteen, at the beginning of my sophomore year at Yale, I said very timidly and shyly to my advisor, 'I want to become a writer, sir.' And he said, 'Well, ah, Knowles, there are only ten people in the country who can support themselves being a writer, so we'll set up your curriculum so that you'll become a teacher.' I thought, I'll show you, you dreary little academic. From that moment, I decided that's the one thing I am going to do if it kills me. And I did."

JOHN KNOWLES was born September 16, 1926, in Fairmont, West Virginia. He received the 1960 William Faulkner Foundation Award and the 1961 Richard and Hilda Rosenthal Award in Fiction from the American Academy of Arts and Letters for *A Separate Peace*. Other novels include *Indian Summer*, *Morning in Antibes*, *Double Vision*, *A Stolen Past*, *The Private Life of Axie Reed*, and *Peace Breaks Out*. He lives in Ft. Lauderdale, Florida.

FT. LAUDERDALE, 1988

Elmore Leonard

"I've always wanted to write, at least since the time I started reading. The major influence was Ernest Hemingway, no question about that. I learned structure from him and what to leave out, but came to see we really didn't share the same attitude about life. He took everything, including himself, so seriously, while I tend to see humor in all kinds of situations. Once I realized that style comes out of attitude I loosened up, sort of let my prose flow with a more natural sound and before long critics were calling me a stylist."

ELMORE "DUTCH" LEONARD was born October 11, 1925, in New Orleans, Louisiana. He has been praised by *Newsweek* as "the greatest crime writer of our time, perhaps ever." Leonard has written over thirty-nine books and has been published in sixteen languages. His highly acclaimed novels include *Glitz*, *Killshot*, *Freaky Deaky* and *Maximum Bob*. *Get Shorty* and *Toshimingo Blues* were produced as films. All were national best-sellers. He lives in Birmingham, Michigan, and North Palm Beach, Florida.

NORTH PALM BEACH, 1992

ROY LICHTENSTEIN

"I decided to go to art school when I was fifteen. It was one subject my high school didn't teach, and I was interested in it. I lived in New York City and I went to museums. I saw a lot of art as a child. I had a little session at being a scientist in my own mind—although I was probably more of an oddball than a scientist. Mostly, I was interested in art.

I drew some charcoal things in the late fifties, in '57 or '58—of Donald Duck and Mickey Mouse. They were still kind of de Kooningesque. I got the idea practically overnight to go from these things to 'Look Mickey' in 1961. It flew in the face of everything I had been taught. I realized that I had been making paintings out of all the good things—trying to hold the composition together with School of Paris brush strokes—and thick and thin paint. I realized that painting isn't just a combination of all the good things you think of."

ROY LICHTENSTEIN was born October 27, 1923, in New York City. Moving from abstract expressionism to cartoons as subject matter in 1961, Lichtenstein began producing the breakthrough paintings that would bring him international acclaim. He utilized new methods of working—painting techniques that imitated and exaggerated the effects of commercial printing. Works by Picasso, Monet, and Matisse, as well as artist's studios, served as subjects for Lichtenstein's paintings. Although his best-known images evolved from comic strips and commercial art, Lichtenstein's treatments and sophisticated versions transcended popular levels of taste. A member of the American Academy of Arts and Letters, Roy Lichtenstein lived in New York City and Southampton, New York; and Captiva Island, Florida. He died September 29, 1997.

CAPTIVA, 1987

Robert Ludlum

"I first decided to become a writer at the age of forty when most people have pretty much decided what they are going to do and have been doing for quite a while. I had been a theatrical producer for a long time after having been an actor in New York. It got to the point where I really felt that the theater in the late-sixties was not the theater that I had been trained for. My wife and I decided that we were going to mark out eighteen months and just see what happened. I started a novel. It was based on a short story I had started ten years before that. I wrote it and a startling thing occurred. It was published and became what is known euphemistically as a bestseller. It was called *The Scarletti Inheritance* and gave me enough money to write my second and third books. That's how it happened in 1971 and I've been writing ever since."

ROBERT LUDLUM was born May 25, 1927, in New York City. He is a bestselling author of over twenty-one novels published in thirty-two languages and forty countries, with worldwide sales exceeding 200 million copies. His works include *The Scarletti Inheritance*, *The Aquitane Progression*, *The Matlock Paper*, *The Apocalypse Watch*, *The Bourne Identity*, *The Bourne Supremacy*, and *The Icarus Agenda*. Robert Ludlum lived in White Plains, New York, and Naples, Florida. He died March 12, 2001.

NAPLES, 1988

ALISON LURIE

"When I was a child, there were few possible occupations for women. Women didn't think of becoming a doctor or a lawyer or a businesswoman or a college professor. Very few thought of becoming a photographer, although there were exceptions. So when I was asked as a child, what I wanted to be when I grew up—I said, 'I'll be a writer,' because I realized that some of the books I loved were written by women and because I loved to tell stories and make up imaginary characters. But it wasn't until I was grown-up that I realized what was involved in being a writer and it wasn't until I was in my thirties that my first novel was accepted and I could call myself more than an amateur."

ALISON LURIE was born September 3, 1926, in Chicago, Illinois, but grew up in the suburbs of New York City. She received the 1985 Pulitzer Prize for her novel, *Foreign Affairs*, which was also nominated for the American Book Award and the Book Critic's Circle Award; it was later made into a television film. Lurie received a Guggenheim Fellowship in 1965 and a Rockefeller Foundation grant in 1967. Her other novels include *Love and Friendship*, *The Nowhere City*, *Imaginary Friends*, *Real People*, *The War Between the Tates*, *Only Children*, *The Truth About Lorin Jones*, and *The Last Resort*. She has also published a collection of short stories, *Women and Ghosts*, and three non-fiction books, *The Language of Clothes*, *Don't Tell the Grownups* (essays on children's literature), and *Familiar Spirits*, a memoir of James Merrill and David Jackson. Alison Lurie is a member of the American Academy of Arts and Letters. She lives in Ithaca, New York, and Key West, Florida.

KEY WEST, 1987

John D. MacDonald

"In 1944 when I was assigned to OSS in the China Burma India Theater, I was restricted as to what I could put in letters to my wife. So I wrote a short story to amuse her. She typed it in proper form and submitted it to Story Magazine, edited by Whitt and Hallie Burnett. They bought it for $25. I learned this when I was discharged at Camp Dix as a Lieutenant Colonel. As I had four months of leave due me, with pay, I decided to take my shot at writing for a living. I was 29."

JOHN D. MACDONALD was born July 24, 1916, in Sharon, Pennsylvania. He wrote 54 novels, 3 non-fiction works, more than 500 magazine stories and articles, and 21 Travis McGee epics. His books sold over 90 million copies worldwide, including the bestsellers *Condominium* and *A Flash of Green* (both produced as films), *The Green Ripper*, *Barrier Island*, and *Slam the Big Door*. One of the last pieces of writing by MacDonald, *Reading for Survival*, is a powerful dialogue between Travis McGee and his friend Meyer on the "terrible isolation of the nonreader." He received the Grand Master Award from the Mystery Writers of America in 1972 and the American Book Award for *The Green Ripper* in 1979. John D. MacDonald lived on Siesta Key, Florida. He died December 28, 1986.

SIESTA KEY, 1983

WILLIAM MANCHESTER

"I can't remember a time when I didn't want to write and, indeed, didn't write. My mother preserved some doggerel I wrote when I was seven years old. I was writing short stories when I was eleven. Writing really is the only thing that I have ever known how to do well.

Apart from the Menken biography, the first four books I published in the 1950s were novels. They were critical successes, but they were not bookstore successes. I couldn't support my family writing fiction so I began writing magazine articles and short stories. Then President Kennedy persuaded me to turn to non-fiction. He argued that the nineteenth century was the golden age of the novel because imaginative events were more interesting than reality then. In the twentieth century, he said, history has turned the other way. Reality has become more exciting, that therefore what people want are tales of what had really happened rather than novels, which were parables of reality.

I was working on my first big non-fiction book, *The Arms of Krupp*, when he was assassinated. His widow and his brother Bob, who knew of our friendship, suggested that I write an account of his death and funeral. That and the Krupp book were published in successive years in the mid-sixties and became my first financial successes."

WILLIAM MANCHESTER was born on April 1, 1922, in Attleboro, Massachusetts. His eighteen books, which have been translated into nineteen languages and Braille, include *Disturber of the Peace: The Life of H.L. Menken*; *The City of Anger*; *The Death of A President: November 20–25, 1963*; *The Glory and the Dream: America 1932–1972*; *American Caesar: Douglas MacArthur, 1880–1964*; *Goodbye Darkness: A Memoir of the Pacific War*; and *The Last Lion: Winston Spencer Churchill* (three volumes). He is a contributor to *Harper's*, *The Atlantic Monthly*, *Esquire*, *The New Yorker*, and *The New York Times Magazine*. His has been a recipient of the Priz International Dag Hammarskjold au Merite Litteraire, five honorary degrees, and a Guggenheim Fellowship. William Manchester lived in Middletown, Connecticut, and on Long Boat Key, Florida. He died June 1, 2004.

LONG BOAT KEY, 1995

CONRAD MARCA-RELLI

"For me, drawing and painting started when I was a child. A good part of my youth was spent in Europe—chiefly in Rome. There I viewed the classical architecture and art that was around me all the time. Because my father traveled, I had a dual-education. By age fifteen, I felt as much at home in Italy as in America as I spoke the languages and was exposed to both cultures. At age seventeen, I joined a private art class in New York associated with Cooper Union that lasted about six months. Essentially, I was self-taught. Besides becoming an artist, I never had any other occupation or ambition.

I was in Mexico in 1950 and I ran out of color, so I started working with paper collages. I found that I was actually simplifying my method of working and I didn't have to wait so long for the paint to dry. I became involved in doing large collages when I got back to the New York studio. I was looking for the forms of negative and positive spaces—to relate one to the other. It was easy to change a shape a hundred times until I got it right. I've been able to do that all my life because to me it's painting, it's no different."

CONRAD MARCA-RELLI was born January 5, 1913, in Boston, Massachusetts. In the early 1950s he turned to collage and became an international master in that medium. Combining oil paint and collage on a large scale, he achieved his signature style of abstract simplicity by juxtaposing large black or ocher shapes on a colorless foundation. A resident of Siesta Key from 1980 until about 1990, he then moved to Wayne, New Jersey, and in 1996 to Parma, Italy. He died August 29, 2000.

SIESTA KEY, 1983

Thomas McGuane

"I always wanted to be a writer. I imagined all writers to be like Rimbaud and
Keats and Stephen Crane, that is, free and vaguely tragic.

What are my suggestions for the governor of Florida? Harry Crews!"

THOMAS MCGUANE was born December 11, 1939, in Wyandotte, Michigan. He is the
author of *The Bushwhacked Piano*, which won the Richard and Hilda Rosenthal Award
from the American Academy of Arts and Letters in 1972, and *Ninety-Two in the Shade*,
which was nominated for the National Book Award in 1974. Other books by McGuane are
The Sporting Club, *Panama*, *Nobody's Angel*, *Something to Be Desired*, *Keep the Change*,
Nothing But Blue Skies, *The Cadence of Grass*, *An Outside Chance: Essays on Sport*, and *To
Skin a Cat*, a collection of stories. McGuane wrote the screenplays for *The Missouri Breaks*,
Tom Horn, and *Ninety-Two in the Shade*, a film he also directed. His stories have appeared
in *Esquire*, *Harper's*, *Playboy*, and *Shenandoah*. A resident of Key West from the late sixties
to the late seventies, he now lives in McLeod, Montana.

KEY WEST, 1986

ROLLIE McKENNA

"In 1948 I was pretty close to deciding on a career in photography, but I'd say in 1950, I'd definitely decided. There were two influences—I was getting my Master's Degree in History of Art with a specialty in Architecture while at Vassar College in 1948 and '49. I took a trip to Europe that first year looking at architecture and I fell in love with the buildings. For the next two years, my mentor Dr. Richard Krautheimer and I, decided that what I should do would be to photograph Italian Renaissance architecture. Then on the *Liberte* en route to Europe, I ran into John Malcolm Brinnin. Although we'd had an introduction by a mutual friend, we took two or three days to look each other up. I think each of us was afraid we'd get stuck with the other. But it was like love at first sight. We've been friends since then and we've worked together a great deal. He really furthered my interest in photographing people."

ROLLIE MCKENNA was born Rosalie Thorne McKenna on November 15, 1918, in Houston, Texas. An internationally celebrated photographer, she is best known for her thoughtful portraits of the writers Dylan Thomas, W. H. Auden, T. S. Eliot, Edith Sitwell, James Merrill, Richard Wilbur, and Elizabeth Bishop, among others. Her books of photography include *Rollie McKenna: A Life in Photography*, *Portrait of Dylan: A Photographer's Memoir*, and *The Modern Poets: An American-British Anthology*. McKenna's work has appeared in periodicals such as *Vogue*, *Harper's Bazaar*, *Look*, *Esquire*, *Newsweek*, and *Time*. Rollie McKenna lived in Northampton, Massachusetts, and Key West, Florida. She died June 14, 2003.

KEY WEST, 1989

JAMES MERRILL

"Although I am a New Yorker, both my parents were born and raised in Florida, my mother in Jacksonville, my father in Green Cove Springs. Both those towns still have corners which the twentieth century seems hardly to have touched. Only last year I spent a night in Jacksonville in the only house left on earth where I could be received by the same dear hostess who made me welcome as a babe in arms. This for me, accordingly, represents the 'real' Florida, as distinguished from the geriatric or economic ghettos proliferating to the south. Key West, when I first began to winter there, struck me as preserving a touch or two of that original innocence: great trees, cracked sidewalks, the sociable cemetery. I hope I disappear before they do.

I began writing in my early teens, but it probably took the interest of some wonderful teachers—as well as the dreamlike ease with which the first poems I sent off to *Poetry* magazine were accepted—to let me feel I might plausibly devote my life to doing what came naturally."

JAMES MERRILL was born March 3, 1926, in New York City. A major American poet, he published over fifteen books including *Water Street*, *Nights and Days*, *The Fire Screen*, *The Yellow Pages*, and *The Changing Light at Sandover*. He was awarded the National Book Award for *Nights and Days* in 1967, the Pulitzer Prize for *Divine Comedies* in 1977, and the National Book Award for *Mirabell* in 1979. Merrill also received the Bollingen Prize, the National Book Critics Circle Award, and was a member of the American Academy of Arts and Letters. In 1990 he was the first recipient of the Rebekah Johnson Bobbitt Prize awarded by the Library of Congress. James Merrill lived in Stonington, Connecticut, and Key West, Florida. He died February 6, 1995.

KEY WEST, 1985

James A. Michener

"I started to write when I was forty years old. I think that to many men of an older age, which I was when I was drafted, military service is a very traumatic experience. In the middle of it you think that if you're ever going to make a change in your civilian life—this is probably the time to do it. Many of my friends became clergymen, went into politics, quit the business they were in, and went into some other business. It was a national experience, I think, of men that age whose lives had been totally disrupted by the war.

I was a very poor boy and it was remarkable that I got an education. My early influences were mostly European—Balzac, Dickens, Dostoevsky. I learned enormously from them. I could have learned just as much from the great American writers, but unfortunately, I did not have instruction or experiences with them."

JAMES ALBERT MICHENER was born of unknown parents on or about February 3, 1907, in New York City. He is one of the world's most popular and beloved writers. His first book, *Tales of the South Pacific*, was published in 1947. It won the Pulitzer Prize and was turned by Rogers and Hammerstein into the renowned Broadway musical, *South Pacific*.

In the fifty-eight years since, Michener wrote forty books, including the bestsellers *The Bridges at Toki-Ri*, *Sayonara*, *Hawaii*, *Centennial*, *The Source*, *Chesapeake*, *Alaska*, *Texas*, and *Recessional*, among others. Michener was decorated with America's highest civilian award, the Presidential Medal of Freedom. While a resident of Florida, James Michener lived in Juno Beach, Coral Gables, and St. Petersburg. Michener spent his last years in Austin, Texas. He died October 16, 1997.

CORAL GABLES, 1988

JULES OLITSKI

"I decided to be an artist, exactly what my life would be, when I saw my grand-mother being lifted into her grave. That I see like it happened five minutes ago. It was a rainy day. Looking around at my stepfather, and my stepbrothers, and the friends of the family—I had this thought, and you know the way young people can sometimes be lacking in compassion and understanding, and I thought I don't want to live the lives that these people live. I want to live the life of someone who creates."

JULES OLITSKI was born March 27, 1922, in Snovsk, USSR. In 1965, he abandoned conventional means of working and began to spray his paint. By gradually spraying selected colors in a subdued manner on top of one another, he produced transparent atmospheric effects. Olitski then incorporated varied lines of color near the edges of his sprayed canvases so that the more conventional components of the painting appeared at the borders. The resulting effects of this new form of painting further established Olitski's reputation as an innovative modern master. In the late seventies, he began utilizing thickly textured surfaces, which were then sprayed, producing a sensuous viewing experience for the spectator. Recently, the artist that critic Clement Greenberg called "the best living painter" is doing small Turneresque pastels and watercolors of sunrises that occur over the water where he lives. In 1969, Olitski became the first living American artist to receive a one-man show at New York's Metropolitan Museum of Art. He lives in Meredith, New Hampshire, and Islamorada, Florida.

ISLAMORADA, 1985

LARRY POONS

"You paint to find out what's in your head so you can look at it. You don't know what's in your head—that's why you paint. All great art is made with that degree of awareness of not knowing what it is you're really doing when you're doing it. You'll find out when you're through. Then you'll play back the tape and hear what you said.

When I was fifteen years old I knew I wanted to be an artist of some sort—a musician, poet, painter. I did them all, but eventually felt I was best for painting. I felt most at home with it."

LARRY POONS was born October 1, 1937, in Tokyo, Japan. In the early 1960s, his paintings were beginning to receive critical attention. By the end of that decade, he was considered one of the young masters of the New York School. After 1970, Poons's methods of working changed and he developed a new way to apply paint. Utilizing a thickly impastoed surface, he throws, in arcs from right to left, the paint from five gallon cans onto the prepared canvas. This allows the opportunity for his color to find its way down the textured, vertically anchored canvas. These paintings are a legacy of abstract expressionism, yet are highly personal in concept and unique in achievement. He lives in New York City, East Durham, New York; and Islamorada, Florida.

ISLAMORADA, 1985

PADGETT POWELL

"As a teenager, I read Norman Mailer's *Advertisements for Myself* and decided it was a pretty good way to go. When, later, it developed I was too small to carry a football, the notion was confirmed: I would have to learn to talk birds out of trees."

PADGETT POWELL was born April 25, 1952, in Gainesville, Florida. His first novel, *Edisto*, was excerpted in *The New Yorker*, nominated for the American Book Award, and named one of the five best books of fiction in 1984 by *Time*. He received a Whiting Foundation Writers' Award in 1986 and the Rome Fellowship in Literature from the American Academy of Arts and Letters in 1987. Powell published his second novel, *A Woman Named Drown*, in 1987 and two collections of short stories, *Typical* in 1991 and *Aliens of Affection* in 1998. He lives in Gainesville, Florida.

GAINESVILLE, 1988

ROBERT RAUSCHENBERG

"It was in the Navy, I guess in 1943 or 1945, when I discovered that everybody couldn't draw. I worked my way through boot camp by making sketches of the other sailors to send home to their wives and their loved ones. I didn't pick up on it immediately. It wasn't until I had a girlfriend in Los Angeles who told me that I was an artist. I was working—either packing bathing suits, or counting buttons, whichever came first. She was from Kansas. That's when I went to the Kansas City Art Institute and I ran full-tilt from then on.

All art, to my way of thinking, is communication through a caring person's observation. Whether it be photography, painting, dancing—the medium is not critical, it's the observation that should be tasted and tested."

ROBERT RAUSCHENBERG was born October 22, 1935, in Port Arthur, Texas. He is often regarded as the most influential artist to react against abstract expressionism. Rauschenberg's imagination and open-minded methods as an artist allow him to combine materials and unrelated subject matter in ways that free the viewer to experience provocative new concepts in art, but in terms that he or she may not have been prepared for.

In addition to his engagements photography, painting, collage, "combines," and "gluts," Rauschenberg is also noted for his work with film, ballet, and theatrical presentations. He is a member of the American Academy of Arts and Letters. Robert Rauschenberg lives on Captiva Island, Florida.

CAPTIVA, 1987

LARRY RIVERS

"I played in bands in the early '40s before I was an artist. I was a saxophone player. We had a job up in Maine and the piano player's wife, who has come down to us now as Jane Freilicher, came up to visit her husband. She was an artist. During the day we'd try different art projects. I got interested in it. One night, that band gig ended and we went back to New York. We both decided to go to Hans Hoffman. We were sort of attracted to each other on many levels. I think a good part of it was the art thing, she wanted to get back into it and I wanted to learn. So I went to school. She was very instrumental in me going to study with Hoffman in 1947 and getting into art and meeting a lot of artists."

LARRY RIVERS was born Yitzroch Loiza Grossberg August 17, 1925, in the Bronx. As a professional saxophonist, he changed his name to Rivers. He began writing poetry, producing sculptures, stage designs, as well as paintings. Rivers utilized abstract expressionism technique, but he incorporated a more figurative approach—old master canvases, historic figures, popular themes and events, often served as subjects for his paintings. His literary collaborators include Kenneth Koch (*When the Sun Tries to Go On*), Frank O'Hara (*Kenneth Koch: A Tragedy*), Terry Southern (*The Donkey and the Darling*), and Arnold Weinstein with whom he co-authored his autobiography, *What Did I Do?* Rivers was a member of the American Academy of Arts and Letters. Larry Rivers lived in New York City, South Hampton, New York; and South Beach, Florida. He died August 14, 2002.

SOUTH BEACH, 1997

JAMES ROSENQUIST

"Painting today, in the technological age, is the ability to put layers and layers of thought on a single canvas so that the energy sort of seeps out of it and people keep seeing things. It's difficult.

I decided to become an artist in 1952. This was because of a natural ability to draw and the urging of Cameron Booth, a distinguished artist and a student of Hans Hoffman, after World War I. When I started, I decided to make pictures of fragments, images that would spill off the canvas instead of recede into it, like a medicine cabinet. I thought each fragment would be identified at a different rate of speed, and that I would paint them as realistically as possible. Then I thought about the kinds of imagery I'd use. I wanted to find images that were a little out of style, but that hadn't reached the point of nostalgia."

JAMES ROSENQUIST was born November 29, 1933, in Grand Forks, North Dakota. Between 1958 and 1960 Rosenquist worked as a sign painter, painting the enormous bill-boards in Times Square while becoming interested in the large paintings of Jackson Pollock and Sam Francis. His experience painting these huge advertisements, involving extreme close-ups of gigantic details of the human face and figure, as well as of industrial objects, supplied the basis for his reverberating views of America's popular culture. He lives in Aripeka, Florida.

ARIPEKA, 1983

Bob Shacochis

"When I was in the first and second grades I was writing plays and producing them for my class. I must have just been hideous. Then for some reason, something happened. It probably wasn't a grand event. But something happened and I went from being that extrovert to a very introverted kid who never opened his mouth and just went into his room and read books. I felt that I had to shut up and escape. It probably was simply the way I was listened to—or rather, not listened to by my family.

I've never decided to become a writer—it's just something that unraveled in my life. Writing allows me to keep myself educated. Whenever I break off for awhile, the sense of feeling stupid is immediate. It's like my intelligence and the education that I have are fragile commodities that can easily diminish and erode or fade without constant maintenance. So that's really why I write; to keep myself educated, for the lifestyle, to be part of the community that I admire, for revenge, for attention—apparently, I have a need for attention."

Bob Shacochis was born September 9, 1951, in West Pittston, Pennsylvania. He won the 1985 National Book Award for his first collection of short stories, *Easy in the Islands*. In 1989, he received the American Academy of Arts and Letters Rome Prize for a subsequent collection of stories, *The Next New World*. Shacochis is also the author of the novel, *Swimming in the Volcano*, which was a finalist for the 1993 National Book Award, and the cookbook, *Domesticity: A Gastronomic Interpretation of Love*. He is a columnist for *GQ* and a contributing editor for *Outside* magazine and *Harper's*. He lives in Tallahassee, Florida.

TALLAHASSEE, 1997

WILFRID SHEED

"I decided to become a writer when I realized I couldn't do anything else. If I had to narrow it down to one influence, it was *The Thurber Carnival* which I read when I got back to England after the war. It had an American sound that I missed and wanted to imitate. I thought, this was the way you write sentences. When I was about eleven, I had discovered a book that contained some John Keats and I was absolutely dazzled and knocked out by it. This in a vague sort of way was what I would like to do if I possibly could. And then the Thurber book gave me a tempo. At that point, all I wanted to do was write some good sentences. I was fifteen and doing a lot of reading. I got polio the year before and had a lot of time on my hands."

Wilfrid John Joseph Sheed was born December 27, 1930, in London, England. A versatile and prolific writer, he has written over fourteen books, three of which were nominated for the National Book Award in Fiction: *Office Politics* (1967), *Max Jamison* (1971), *People Will Always Be Kind* (1974). He was also nominated for a Book Critics Circle Award in Criticism: *Essays in Disguise* (1990). Other titles by Sheed include *Muhammad Ali: A Portrait in Words and Photographs*, *Transatlantic Blues*, and *In Love With Daylight: A Memoir of Recovery*. He served as drama critic for *Commonweal* (1964–1967), as movie critic for *Esquire* (1966–1970), and as a columnist for *The New York Times Book Review* (1970–1973). Sheed received a Guggenheim Fellowship and an award in literature from the American Academy of Arts and Letters in 1971. He lives in Sag Harbor, New York, and Key West, Florida.

KEY WEST, 1996

Isaac B. Singer

"I will tell you, my childhood years in Warsaw were the most important to me as a writer. Many times, in my memories, I have returned to Number 10 Krochmalna Street where I lived as a little boy. It was there that I was introduced to the struggles and the richness of human nature. My orientation and my feelings are still a result of my first thirty years of life in Poland. For me as a writer, the Poland of my youth still exists."

ISAAC BASHEVIS SINGER was born Icek-Hersz Zynger July 14, 1904 in Radzymin, Poland. The son and grandson of rabbis, he broke from strict orthodox tradition and began writing at age seventeen, following in the footsteps of his older brother, Israel Joshua. Singer came to America in 1935 and became a citizen in 1943. He received practically every award the literary world has to give, including: the Nobel Prize for Literature in 1978, National Book Awards for *A Day of Pleasure*, 1970, and for *A Crown of Feathers*, 1974, and the Gold Medal for Fiction from the American Academy of Arts and Letters, 1989. He wrote over 30 titles—short stories, novels, children's books and memoirs—all in Yiddish, the language of his childhood in Warsaw's Jewish Ghetto district. His short novel, *Yentil, The Yeshiva Boy*, was produced as a play and film. Isaac Bashevis Singer lived in New York City and Surfside, Florida. He died July 24, 1991.

SURFSIDE, 1988

Patrick D. Smith

"I first decided to become a writer during my junior high school years. This was in the late 1930s and early '40s. Back then there was no TV or other such forms of entertainment, so I read books—many books. This influenced me to want to write."

Patrick Davis Smith was born October 8, 1927, in Mendenhall, Mississippi. He was nominated for the Pulitzer Prize for both *Angel City*, which was produced as a film, and *Forever Island*, which has been published in forty-six countries. Other books by Smith include *The River Is Home*, *The Beginning*, and *Allapatah*. His sixth and best-known novel, *A Land Remembered* was also nominated for a Pulitzer and received the Florida Historical Society's Tebeau Prize for most outstanding Florida historical novel. He is a popular lecturer in the United States and abroad and participated in several cultural exchanges with the former Soviet Union. He lives on Merritt Island, Florida.

MERRITT ISLAND, 1985

SYD SOLOMON

"I had a leaning before the war. I leaned on bars, I leaned on golf clubs, I leaned on a bit of talent to do almost any art job. After W.W. II (and five bronze stars later) I knew that I was wanting most to become part of the great American development of abstract expressionism.

My reveries, my visual memories, my own tentativeness, all contribute to subject matter. All, so difficult to discuss since it has now become more than ever an expanded part of a ceaseless reaction of moving forms in a horizonless playground. There, shadow and light embrace color shades. Sometimes caught in a soft mellow atmosphere—and other times, in a swift threatening wave of space that is fluid, not structural, certainly imitating the sea and the orbit of objects that press around it. Perhaps this can be my own relationship to the cosmos."

Syd Solomon was born July 12, 1917, in Uniontown, Pennsylvania. A pioneer in the abstract expressionistic movement, his work has received international attention and acclaim since the movement began a few decades ago. Solomon's paintings are characterized by a sensitive interplay of color and light—evocative forms that reflect his vision of the tension, and changes in mood arising between land and the sea. Regarded as a "one man chamber of culture," he arrived in Sarasota on January 1, 1946, and significantly contributed to the culture of that area. Syd Solomon lived in Sagaponack, Long Island, and Siesta Key, Florida. He died January 28, 2004.

SIESTA KEY, 1983

Robert Stone

"I think very early on I wanted to be a writer—if I could be one, if I could make my living that way. The first piece of writing I ever had published was something I did in high school. Then when I was in the Navy, I started trying to write fiction. I think I was really influenced by the earlier generation of great moderns like Hemingway and Steinbeck and Scott Fitzgerald. I read them during my high school years, but not as part of my studies. It was work like theirs that I aspired to—that was the work I admired."

Robert Stone was born August 21, 1937, in Brooklyn, New York. His first novel, *A Hall of Mirrors*, won a William Faulkner Foundation Award in 1968. *Dog Soldiers* received a National Book Award in 1975 and *A Flag for Sunrise* won the Los Angeles Times Book Prize in 1982. He is also the author of *Children of Light*, *Damascus Gate*, *Outerbridge Reach*, *Bay of Souls*, and a collection of stories, *Bear and His Daughter*. Other honors include a Guggenheim Fellowship, an award from the American Academy of Arts and Letters, the John Dos Passos Prize for Literature, and a National Endowment for the Arts Fellowship. In 1984, he received the Mildred and Harold Strauss Livings from the American Academy of Arts and Letters. Both *A Hall of Mirrors* and *Dog Soldiers* were made into major films. Stone is a member of the American Academy of Arts and Letters. He lives in West Port, Connecticut, and Key West, Florida.

KEY WEST, 1993

PETER TAYLOR

"I wrote stories as a child. My first serious effort came in 1936 when I was studying with Alan Tate at Rhodes College in Memphis. I sent two of my stories to Robert Penn Warren at *Southern Review* my freshman year and they were rejected.

I don't think of myself as a regional writer. I write about people under certain circumstances—in a particular place at a particular time, but then that's what art is about—the relation of the particular to the general."

Peter Taylor was born January 8, 1917, in Trenton, New Jersey. Admired for his finely detailed portraits of Southern aristocracy, Taylor received the Pulitzer Prize and the Ritz Paris Hemingway Award in 1987 for his novel *A Summons to Memphis*. He was often called America's greatest living short story writer. Vivid masterpieces of that form appear in *The Old Forest and Other Stories*, which won the PEN/Faulkner Award for best work of fiction, 1985. Other books by Taylor include *A Long Fourth and Other Stories*, *Happy Families Are All Alike*, *In The Miro District*, *The Oracle at Stoneleigh Court*, the novels *A Woman of Means*, and *In the Tennessee Country*, and four books of plays. His work was published in *Best American Short Story* and O. Henry collections and conform to the author's mandate that "compression is everything." Peter Taylor lived in Charlottesville, Virginia, and Gainesville, Florida. He died November 2, 1994.

KEY WEST, 1988

JERRY N. UELSMANN

"I more or less entered art through a back door. I was interested in photography at a very early age. In high school it filled a lot of needs for me. After graduation, I thought I wanted to be a commercial photographer and I went to the Rochester Institute of Technology. It was there that I had some rather key intersections. I was blessed with encountering Ralph Hattersley, Beaumont Newhall, and Minor White. I had a very limited perspective on what photography could be previous to encountering these gentlemen. I became excited by the idea that you could make images for personal reasons.

To me the camera is like a license to explore. When I photograph I become a sort of visual archaeologist or anthropologist and I don't try to complete the image at the camera. For me, the creative moment occurs in the darkroom."

Jerry Norman Uelsmann was born June 11, 1934, in Detroit, Michigan. He received a Guggenheim Fellowship in 1967 and a Photographer's Fellowship from the National Endowment for the Arts in 1972. Uelsmann's best known works are the dreamlike, often haunting landscapes he creates by expertly exposing and blending a number of selected negatives to form a single image. His provocative, highly personal photographs are well-crafted composites of Florida's mysterious swamps, exotic foliage, secluded beaches, bare trees, and overgrown, deserted buildings. He lives in Gainesville, Florida.

GAINESVILLE, 1988

RICHARD WILBUR

"I had always written poems, from time to time, since early childhood; I decided that I was doomed to be a poet when, in 1946, a friend sent my poems to a New York publisher and the publisher wrote me to say that he wanted to do a book of mine. When people ask to publish you, or when readers write to say that your poems have made a difference in their lives, it becomes clear that you must call yourself a poet.

What made me want to write poems in the first place? My enjoyment of the poems of others. There was never one great influence upon me; starting with nursery rhymes, I have always taken pleasure from a large number and variety of poems and poets."

Richard Wilbur was born March 1, 1921, in New York City. Widely honored as a poet, translator, and lecturer, he served as Poet Laureate of the United States from 1987–1988. In 1956, Wilbur's words were sung on Broadway, set to Leonard Bernstein's musical score of *Candide*. He received the Edna St. Vincent Millay Memorial Award, the National Book Award, the Pulitzer Prize for his third volume of poetry, *Things of This World* (1957), and the Pulitzer Prize in 1989 for *New and Collected Poems*. Wilbur's translations of Moliere are considered classics—his rendering of the Moliere comedies won a Tony Award in 1994. He was the recipient of the Bollingen Prize in 1961, the Shelley Memorial Award in 1973, and the National Medal of the Arts in 1994. Wilbur was a State Department Cultural Exchange Representative in 1961 and Chancellor of the American Academy of Arts and Letters from 1976 to 1978 and 1980 to 1981. His critically acclaimed *Collected Poems, 1943–2004* was released in 2005. He lives in Cummington, Massachusetts, and Key West, Florida.

KEY WEST, 1988

CHARLES WILLEFORD

"I had always wanted to write. I started writing poetry when I was a kid. When I got into the Army I didn't do much of anything for a long time, but then I got on a sidetrack and I started painting. I was painting for about eight years. I went to the Los Angeles Art Center, studied in Lima, Peru, and I finally decided that I wasn't going to make it as a painter. I never did develop my own style so I gave that up. And that's when I turned to writing. If you're a creative person you've got to find the right niche. Although I've been able to use what I know about painting in my writing. I've written a couple novels where the hero was a painter or an art critic. So I've been able to use this information and it also helped me to look at things."

Charles Willeford III was born January 2, 1919, in Little Rock, Arkansas. He was an actor, poet, and the author of the Hoke Moseley mystery series. His engaging memoir, *I Was Looking for a Street*, recounts his wanderings out West as a teenage vagabond during the depression and is a companion volume to his autobiographical *Something about a Soldier*. Willeford wrote a book of poetry, *Proletarian Laughter*, and a book of literary criticism entitled *New Forms of Ugly: The Immobilized Man in Modern Literature*. His novels include *Cockfighter*, *New Hope for the Dead*, *The Burnt Orange Heresy*, *Miami Blues*, which was produced as the film *Sideswipe*, and *The Way We Die Now*. Charles Willeford lived in South Miami, Florida. He died March 27, 1988.

SOUTH MIAMI, 1988

JOY WILLIAMS

"When did I decide to be a writer? I don't know. No kindly or compelling vision appeared. I do know that my first library card was very, very important to me. I was an only child growing up in Maine and my father was a minister. Maybe that's why I became a writer."

Joy Williams was born February 11, 1944, in Chelmsford, Massachusetts. Her stories have appeared in *The New Yorker*, *Paris Review*, and *Esquire*, as well as the *Best American Short Story* and O. Henry collections. Her first novel, *State of Grace*, was nominated for the National Book Award in 1974. She is also the author of the novels *The Changeling*, *Breaking and Entering*, and *The Quick and the Dead*, as well as three collections of short stories: *Taking Care*, *Escapes*, and *Honored Guest*. Joy Williams's *Guide to the Florida Keys and Key West* was called "one of the best travel books ever written" by *Traveler* magazine. *Ill Naturé*, a book of essays, was a finalist for the National Book Critics Circle Award for criticism. She is the recipient of a Guggenheim Fellowship, a grant from the National Endowment for the Arts, the Mildred and Harold Strauss Living Award from the American Academy of Arts and Letters 1993, and the Rea Award for the Short Story 1999. She divides her time between Tuscon, Arizona and Key West, Florida.

SIESTA KEY, 1983

*"Every child is an artist.
The problem is how to remain an artist
once he grows up."*

Pablo Picasso

CONVERSATIONS 1

When did you first come to Florida?

What were your first impressions?

What aspects of your work have been affected as a result of your time in the state?

EDWARD ALBEE

I was an orphan and was adopted by the Albees, who were sort of a moneyed family. They had a house in Larchmount about 20 miles outside of New York City. In the winters they came down to Palm Beach and lived with Grandmother, who had a house on the ocean. From the time I was a baby, I spent all of my winters in Palm Beach. Until I left home when I was eighteen or nineteen and went off on my own.

I didn't come back to Florida very much until I started having plays done at the Coconut Grove Playhouse. Once I started being a practicing playwright and had enough money to travel as I liked, I spent a lot of time in the Caribbean. I had a big loft in New York City, a house out on Montauk on the ocean, and I wanted a place in the sun because the older I get, the more warmth I like. I'd gotten rather bored with being a houseguest all the time. I didn't want to buy in the Caribbean—it's so unpredictable there and it takes such a long time to get anywhere. I discovered the South Grove by this point, which is sort of a jungle and a nice quiet place. I can get down here from New York City just about as quickly as I can drive to my house out in Montauk. This seemed very sensible. When I first came down here people asked, "Why don't you get a condo-minium?" But I can't imagine living in one when you can live in a jungle.

Probably more from growing up here a quarter of the year. Those were the formative years, those were the impressionable years, but what aspects of my work specifically? I don't know. I do know that of my twenty-six plays, four or five of them have been set on a beach. And I think it has something to do with the Florida beaches—I wouldn't be surprised. I love walking on the beach when I'm down here. I do it at my house on Montauk. And I did that as a kid on Palm Beach, of course. There used to be beaches in Palm Beach, but now they've all eroded.

RICHARD ANUSZKIEWICZ

I first visited Florida in March 1971. My first impression of Florida was how different it is from any other state. I particularly enjoyed the subtropical landscape.

Aspects of work affected—color.

ANN BEATTIE

The first time I ever came to Florida for any amount of time, other than just passing through briefly on a car trip with my parents as a child, was when I was in high school. My mother and a friend of hers used to bring me and my best friend down to Miami during Easter vacation. We're talking Miami in the '60s. I loved it. It was "other." It was sunny. It looked like people were having fun. I never thought I'd live here.

Things that seem conspicuous to me—visual images that I retain might, in some later time period, appear in my works of fiction. In other words, having first come to Key West in about 1982, I'm not so sure that if something is based in Key West now, it's because I'm living here. My feeling is that it might be anyway. I've had a kind of in-and-out relationship with the place. When I write fiction, what I'm trying to do is to find a place to root the story, rather than the other way around.

JOHN MALCOLM BRINNIN

I first came to Florida in 1942.

Save for what was left of old St. Augustine and what was ostentatiously new in Palm Beach, the state seemed a wasteland of Depression-era suburbs that had lost their moorings and drifted south.

Visits over the next ten years or so modified this impression. I began to understand the audacity of "classic" Miami as represented by the Roney Plaza and the Biltmore; realized that the interconnected Keys were more than the abstractions suggested by WPA posters; and, as a guest in the Cross Creek home

*When did you first
come to Florida?*

*What were your first
impressions?*

*What aspects of your
work have been
affected as a result of
your time in the state?*

of Marjorie Kinnan Rawlings, slept on a corn shuck mattress and otherwise sensed for myself the pastoral reality of "old" Florida.

What aspects of my work have been affected as a result of my time in Florida? None—except for a card (AARP) carrying member of the gerontocracy's sharper memories of years in other places.

PHILIP BURTON

It was extraordinary. It must have been in the early '60s. I was on one of my lecture tours. I had given a lecture in Mexico City on the Friday, and my next lecture was in Miami on the Monday. I had a friend in Key West and he asked me to come and spend the weekend here. The weather was perfect; the people I met were so friendly. It was a wholly delightful experience. I couldn't wait to come back.

I had a very serious heart attack in 1969, followed by another one in 1970 not quite so serious. The doctors told me I should never spend a winter in the cold North because cold weather is bad for the heart since it thickens the blood. So there was only one place.

As far as Key West affecting my work—in the special way this marvelous weather and this charming community have contributed to an atmosphere in which I can gather my thoughts and write freely.

PHILIP CAPUTO

My first sight of Florida took place in 1961, when I joined the annual undergraduate pilgrimage to Ft. Lauderdale. My initial impression, apart from the usual ones of palm trees, sand and sea, was the coeds whom I'd seen bundled up on Northern campuses looked terrific in bikinis. I revisited the state in 1976, spending about two months in Key West, whose ambience struck me more as Caribbean or West Indian than North American. I've lived here, off and on, since 1977.

Have any aspects of my work been affected by my living in Florida? None that I know of.

JOHN CHAMBERLAIN

I first came to Florida in 1969. Then I moved here to get away from Connecticut—that was about 1980. That was before I learned Florida has the third highest incidence of alcoholism in the country. That was really something to come here for.

My first impressions—I liked the flora in Florida.

Everything affects everything else. You're affected, and your work is affected by everything that you're exposed to—to what degree is something else, to what condition is something else—everything is affected, whether you realize it at the time or not. It's the same way when you find something that's very marvelous and you've never seen it before. The next time you see it, it's not as marvelous as it used to be because you've already discovered it.

Art is unprecedented information. I prefer to think it occurs by approaching an idea with an interest that disappears into what's emerging next—something unknown. What I don't know is what I'm after, whether it's 1957 or 1987, whether it's Southampton or Sarasota.

JOHN CIARDI

I visited Florida while on lecture tours in the early 1950s. Following a term as poet-in-residence at the University of Florida in 1973, Judith and I started coming to Key West. We stayed in a shack. After a few seasons of being cramped as recruits, we decided to build a house here—in the same compound as the Wilburs. We moved into the new house in 1979 and continue to spend the winters surrounded by drowsy cats and old friends.

*When did you first
come to Florida?*

*What were your first
impressions?*

*What aspects of your
work have been
affected as a result of
your time in the state?*

My impressions of Key West are of a green paradise—the sun is bright, the days tropical, the shrimp are sweet, and a sea breeze blows in from Cuba, which is only 90 miles away. Garbage trucks carry signs that read: FREE SNOW REMOVAL.

I always seem to come to Florida with work to be done, but I have written a short piece about the place: *Audit at Key West*.

HARRY CREWS

I first came to Florida when I was six. We were migrant farmers. Dirt poor. And as we did when times got bad, when there was not enough money to put shirts on our backs or food on the table, we'd come down to Jacksonville to find work. Actually, we came selling our sweat because that was all we had to sell—we were without special skills of any kind.

My first impression of Florida was that it was another form of madness, with a faint taint of gasoline.

I've used places in Florida in at least a dozen of my books—*Naked in Garden Hills, The Gypsy's Curse, All We Need of Hell, The Knockout Artist, Body, Car, Scar Lover, Karate Is a Thing of the Spirit*, and *Celebration*, among others.

And unless your senses are entirely dead, anyone can see Florida is a self-contained madness. But it seems to work extremely well for certain people like graphic artists, photographers, writers—especially the ones who are extremely mad because they are, and always have been, the best artists.

ANNIE DILLARD

Fort Lauderdale has a wonderful park in the middle of the city. Every year I stayed with my grandmother in nearby Pompano Beach. When I was fourteen, I learned about the park. Daily my grandmother dropped me off there; I packed a lunch, a notebook, and a bird book. There I saw coots and gallinules—together, just as in the field guide's taxonomy. The binoculars banged on my skinny ribs. One day, I got the courage to ask a ranger where to find the smooth-billed aris.

The park had the only breeding population in the US. "At the dump," he said, and they were.

The Gulf Stream comes closest to the US coast at Ft. Lauderdale. Tropical strays blow onto the beaches: by-the-wind sailors and Portuguese men-o'-war. Sharks patrol the river mouth. I loved it all—the hard rain.

I guess I got interested in marine life there; I certainly read *At the Edge of the Sea* and *Under the Sea Wind* several times, that March when I was fourteen. Fondly I imagined myself as a lone, courageous naturalist. But I did that wherever I was, even in Pittsburgh, where I grew up.

We bought a house here in April 1994. Now many of our friends come to Key West. It's awfully good to live among people who spend time the same absurd way we do.

MARJORY STONEMAN DOUGLAS

My first memory of Florida was being held up to pick an orange in the gardens of the Tampa Bay Hotel. I was four years old. I remember the brilliance of the light—the wonderful quality of the light. Then I moved to Florida in 1915 and got a job reporting, on my father's paper, the *Miami Herald.* I loved everything about Florida—the climate, the openness, the wonderful landscape of the bay and the back country.

All my work was dictated by the fact of my being in Florida. I worked for six years on the *Herald* and retired from that to be a freelance writer. I've lived in this house since 1926.

The great problem in Florida is the population explosion. I'm afraid that by the year 2000 there are going to be many more people than there are today. I think that is a constant menace to the future of the environment of the state. People come flooding in and so many don't know or care, really, very much about the unique nature of Florida. They constantly have to be told what are the dangers, and liabilities, and what we're trying to preserve. It's a constant struggle, but I don't think it's entirely hopeless. As a matter of fact, I'm neither optimistic

When did you first
come to Florida?

What were your first
impressions?

What aspects of your
work have been
affected as a result of
your time in the state?

nor pessimistic about it, I say it's *got* to be done! We've got to save the Kissimmee-Okeechobee Everglades basin because if we don't—we won't have any rainfall. Our rainfall largely comes from Everglades evaporation. Without rainfall, Florida is going to be a desert. People have got to learn about our water problems and do things about them, or go and live somewhere else.

My suggestion to the governor of Florida—pay immediate attention to the restoration of the Kissimmee-Okeechobee-Everglades Basin, with special attention to the clean-up of Lake Okeechobee.

RICHARD EBERHART

I first saw Florida as a tourist, and that was a while ago, at about the time I was in my early twenties. I think it was the lushness, and the tall trees, and the sea coast, and the heat. All of these sensuous qualities.

My book *Florida Poems* has only sixteen poems, I think. One was called "Itchetucknee," a rather beautiful universal poem about the Itchetucknee current and the human being. The Itchetuknee was so beautiful when Betty and I used to go out there. It has pure water coming up that is lucid. If you are a swimmer, you can look down and see for 20 feet just as clear as day. I went back there last summer and it was just miserable, absolutely disgusting. It was so dirty, it was so unpretty—it was corrupted. It wasn't the same-looking place at all.

I recognize the fact that locale has meant something to me because I have not only written a book of Florida poems, I've also written a book of Maine poems. I guess the answer is yes, locale is a fact of existence and you obviously absorb things from one part of the country that you wouldn't from another.

DICK FRANCIS

The first time we came was 1974. We came over to the Hialeah blood stock sales in Miami and stayed for a week. We went out to the sales every night, spent the days on the beach. We were doing research for a book which I was writing at that time called *Knockdown*, which was about blood stock sales. Then between 1974 and 1980, Mary's health deteriorated. Asthma developed with her. When the weather gets cold she seizes right up. So we had to find somewhere where it was warm to spend winters. A friend of ours, who lived in Maryland, said that if you're going to go anywhere in America you must go to Ft. Lauderdale. The weather there is better than anywhere in the whole USA. We came over for ten days or two weeks to look for apartments and for properties. We eventually decided to settle here in 1983 and we've been here ever since. It's a good place for writing stories.

I don't get as many telephone interruptions here as I did in England. I find this much more suitable for writing than living in England. The people nowadays say the books are better. I think it's because I can give more uninterrupted time to them. I find it beneficial for writing here—sitting off in sun looking at the ocean. Plots come into your mind. I think they probably come better here now, than they did in England.

MARILYN FRENCH

I didn't like Florida when I first came here. I came with my parents. I came to look for an apartment for them because they liked coming down here. I thought I'd buy it and I'd stay in it a little and then they could use it. I fully intended, when I got this place, to give them the master bedroom and I'd take the little guest room for myself because I didn't think that I would spend much time here. I wasn't here very long before I looked out at the lake, and the ocean, and the sky, and the herons going by and I thought, gee—, and I was quite seduced. They never got the big bedroom.

I've set some scenes down here, but I don't think being in Florida has affected my work. Florida is not any different than the rest of the United States, really. I'm writing about womens' experience which is the same everywhere. It's the same in Japan, it's the same in Africa—maybe the details are different, but the experience is the same.

*When did you first
come to Florida?*

*What were your first
impressions?*

*What aspects of your
work have been
affected as a result of
your time in the state?*

DUANE HANSON

I came to Florida in August 1965. My first impression wasn't too good because a
big hurricane appeared suddenly, shortly after I arrived. I got a job here at Miami
Dade Community College, north campus. I was assistant professor of Art there
for four years. I taught sculpture, ceramics, and art history. It was when I was
there that I ran into my particular type of realism—did some experimentation,
did a small figure that was put in a show. It had a terrific reaction. A real good
reaction for the fact that somebody was working in realism at that time, especially in sculpture. Then I began working with life-size figures. In 1967, to protest
the war in Vietnam, I did a group of four dead soldiers. Also during that time—a
motorcycle accident victim, a race-riot composed of seven figures. It was about
showing the sociological horrors of the '60s.

The illusionist type of work with which I'm still involved is a complicated
procedure of using different materials to fool the eye. I'm not really interested in
trickery, that's a side-product of this whole effect. I'm more interested in making
convincing sculptures where the forms all relate one to another and look right.
That the figure I choose has an impact to the viewer. To communicate my feelings about a society that has a lot of frustration and fatigue running around,
concerns about fuel for the future, inflation, wars, pollution—the things we hear
about day-to-day and want to forget about, but they're always there. We're
affected by this publicly, and inwardly we reflect that, when we have a moment to
ourselves.

Florida is a wonderful place for me because the subject matter is so varied.
I've mined the area over and over. I've used up all my relatives and friends, and
friends of friends. Florida has a great number of chubby people who make great
sculptures. The Florida native is good sculptural material because he, or she, is
not burdened with excessive clothing and often goes around half nude.

JOHN HERSEY

We were invited to join the Wilburs and the Ciardis in a "compound" here in Key West in 1975. My first trip down was to look at the houses that we might convert to form the compound. My impression was of a house that was on it's last legs. It turned out to be full of termites and was inhabited by some very happy hippies. It was a mess. But after some repairs, it's turned out to be a very, very cheerful home to be in.

I think that the brightness of the light here must have cast some shadows in what I put down on paper. I feel a sense of being lifted by the light here. It makes a big difference in my way of doing work.

We've lived too fast in my lifetime. We've consumed without thinking about the consequences of our consumption. I'm afraid greed has been one of the great diseases of my time. Here in Key West, we live near the crest of Solares Hill, which is 16 feet above sea level, they say. But there's a mountain up here on Stock Island which we call "Mt. Trashmore." It is an accumulation of garbage put there since, I think, the 1920s. It's a monument to carelessness and thoughtlessness about our future. It has apparently caused some grief, too. We had a higher incidence here of multiple sclerosis than any community in the country. Several of the nurses in the hospital, which happens to be located right next to Mt. Trashmore, have come down with multiple sclerosis. So I think that we are now beginning to see some of the costs of our carelessness and our greed. With some care and thought, it may be possible to clean up some of our worst follies, but we've got to be thinking about these things very quickly. I feel that, particularly strongly, because I now have four grandchildren and I want them to live in a world where they can breathe the air, and drink the water, and eat the food without always thinking of dangers that there are to what they're doing.

*When did you first
come to Florida?*

*What were your first
impressions?*

*What aspects of your
work have been
affected as a result of
your time in the state?*

CARL HIAASEN

Florida has always been my home and it's like no other place in the union. I don't mean that just for the natural beauty, which is breathtaking—between the oceans, and the Everglades, and the Keys, and the Panhandle—it is incredibly diverse, probably as much as California, but also in terms of the sheer weirdness of the characters it attracts.

Florida is the reason for my work, I think. It's true, you have to write about what you know, what concerns you, what bothers you. The characters here are what appeal to me because my books subsist on weird characters. Florida is a place that attracts, and always has—going back to the turn of the century, people that are either after something, meaning money, or running from something, meaning the law. That's who come here. This place is a tremendous magnet, not just for dope dealers, but for white-collar criminals and scammers who come down and prey on the elderly and resident population. If you're a con man, or crook, or slime ball—you might as well be down here. The weather is nicer than Jersey.

EVAN HUNTER

I first came to Florida in 1975. I loved it then, and I love it now.

I have used Florida settings in a couple of my books.

DONALD JUSTICE

I was born in Miami.

On my return to Florida in 1982, for the first year or two, I was quite lifted up and excited by the landscape and the atmosphere in general. This brought back to me, it seemed, vague childhood recollection and a kind of generalized nostalgia which I valued. That has diminished over the last few years and Florida now seems just about like any other place. But for a couple of years there, it was particularly interesting to me as one coming home, so to speak. Now I'm thinking, wouldn't it be nice to live in California.

I have written several poems about Miami—*Memory of a Porch, Miami, 1942; A Winter Ode to the Old Men of Lummus Park, Miami, Florida;* and *Thinking About the Past.* I have also written about some of the changes that have taken place there in a short story, "The Artificial Moonlight."

WILLIAM KING

I was born here. Florida is a great place for kids. We lived on the East Coast. I was born in Jacksonville and we moved down as the land boom continued. My father was a civil engineer involved in reclaiming islands and draining swamps. We settled in Coconut Grove, finally.

Most of my imagery comes from these palm trees with the long stems and the leaves up on the top. The climate has a lot to do with it—where you're sort of hatched and formed. Florida nights are wonderful, you never forget something like that; daytime, standing on the bay; the Florida weather…I know that stays in the imagery somehow. But the palm trees, I think, have the most to do with it—the way they look.

JAMES KIRKWOOD

I first came to Key West, which was when I first came to Florida, in about 1965. In a way, I don't connect Key West all that much with the rest of Florida. It's unique. When I saw other parts of Florida it occurred to me that if I were dropped down blindfolded and landed in Key West, I would never think I was in Florida—some strange island perhaps.

My impression of Key West was that it was full of a bewitched atmosphere and more "characters" than I could imagine landing in one place. It's one of those end-of-the-line places that attract neurotic, creative souls who never seem to be able to pull their lives together, so they try Provincetown or San Francisco

*When did you first
come to Florida?*

*What were your first
impressions?*

*What aspects of your
work have been
affected as a result of
your time in the state?*

or Venice (California) and finally, Key West. It's got its own brand of tacky charm.

For some weird reason, being in Key West unlocks my imagination, lets my subconscious take over much more than when I'm elsewhere, New York for instance. Perhaps it's because I feel a bit cut off from the real world here. And that is good. The real world can be a terrible intruder when one is writing. Again I have to say there's something intangible in the air—just being here. I know this is true because I've exchanged opinions with so many other writers who live or have lived in Key West and we all feel the same way about the place. It's odd that I've never, yet, written anything directly about Florida or Key West. I feel that will come in time though.

JOHN KNOWLES

My mother and my Aunt Beaulah used to come and spend part of the winters in a riverside hotel on Las Olas Boulevard in Ft. Lauderdale. If I was going away in the winter, I would go somewhere like Egypt because I felt that was what a writer should do, and I was right, in a sense. I was some kind of a travel snob and I felt that Florida was for my mother and Aunt Beaulah. Actually, I first came here to get back in shape at the spa at Palm Aire in Pompano Beach. I came to see mother here in Ft. Lauderdale and saw it wasn't just for old ladies, which was a silly idea in the first place on my part. There are all kinds of people in Ft. Lauderdale. It's a very attractive community. The spring-break thing is kind of a bad rap that Ft. Lauderdale has been having. It's a community that's getting culturally alive. I love the canals, I'm crazy about the water, and boats, and surf, and beach—so here I am.

If I live long enough and if I'm healthy enough, eventually, I'm sure I'll use Florida as a setting for stories or a novel, because that's the way I work. I always start with a place I know well. I simply haven't been here long enough to use it as yet.

ELMORE LEONARD

The first time I came to Florida was in 1950. I loved everything about it. It had a much different look then. There were a lot more of those frame cottages that you'd see along the coast—the Kester cottages, I think they were called. Now, of course, there's that wall of condominiums all the way up the Gold Coast. We would come to the Pompano Beach-Ft. Lauderdale area throughout the '50s, till finally, in the late 60s, I bought a place for my mother. My mother was living in New Orleans where all of us came from. She wasn't too happy there. The neighborhood which she was in should have been condemned. So I bought a motel for her in the late sixties—'68 I think it was. She came down and ran the motel and her sister moved from New Orleans shortly after that to live with her. It didn't make any money. In fact, it cost more to operate than it made, but it kept my mother busy and she was very happy doing that. Until about '84 or '85 when she was getting too old to run it so she moved in with my sister in Little Rock and we sold the place. Then in 1989 we bought this apartment in North Palm Beach, in the marina.

Everybody in advertising is an expert just as everyone in the motion picture business is an expert. That's why I quit writing movies, for the same reason I quit writing ad copy—you're working for someone. When I write a book my goal is to write something that pleases me. I'm the only one I have to please. Whether my book is set in Detroit or South Florida or Italy, it's going to have the same sound. It's going to have my style. It's going to have characters moving the story along as much as possible. In South Florida there's a wonderful mix of people—from Palm Beach down into the Keys. You've got high contrast in the types of people and in the way they live. From the high society of the Palm Beach area down to Haitian, Cuban, Latin enclaves around Miami. There's a certain amount of crime that appeals to me in that Miami area. I didn't use the Cubans coming in 1959. But in 1979 and 1980, the Mariel boat lift, I jumped on that and had a character come off a boat and figure prominently in the story. I like that Latin American sound

*When did you first
come to Florida?*

*What were your first
impressions?*

*What aspects of your
work have been
affected as a result of
your time in the state?*

and the color that's down here and I have used South Florida settings in at least nine of my books.

ROY LICHTENSTEIN

The first time I came to Florida I was in the army. I was on furlough and I visited my folks who were in Sarasota. I was based in Chicago and I think it must have been 1944.

We first heard about Captiva through Bob Rauschenberg. We came down and rented a house in 1978 or '79. That was my second time in Florida. Now, I try to get down here to our own house around the end of the year. There are fewer distractions here than in Southampton or in New York City. The phone doesn't ring as much and I am free to walk on the beach or roam around in my own jungle.

I think there was some Florida influence on the brush stroke landscapes. At first, I did landscapes with cartoon brush strokes. Recently, I use a combination of real brush strokes and cartoon brush strokes mixed in the same painting to make landscapes. I think they may have had their origin here.

ROBERT LUDLUM

I had first come to Florida years ago. My wife, who was a superb actress, was in a show at the Coconut Grove Theater with Margaret Truman and Jack Klugman which I produced. Then years later, I developed a minor kind of arthritic condition that could not take the cold. We decided to look down in Florida, in terms of having a home here for at least part of the year when it was terribly cold up north. Three people, who did not know each other prior to our coming down here, in three successive days, asked if we'd seen Naples. After the third one, we thought of that as an omen. We grabbed a plane and came down here. We both just looked at each other and said, "Hey, this is it!" That was in 1983. We first decided we would be here about four months out of the year. We're now here seven months each year.

I think you tend to become a little more introspective down here. Maybe it's the climate, maybe it's the beauty of where we live—I don't know. I just know that I enjoy working in Florida enormously. How can you help it? You get finished scribbling and you go out and walk this marvelous beach for a couple of hours and you get your head unshredded.

ALISON LURIE

I first came to Key West in 1978, just by accident, and bought a house here in the following year. Friends of mine, Jimmy Merrill and David Jackson, had taken a house here. They couldn't get down for the first two weeks so on an impulse, I sublet it from them. I came down and was amazed mostly because it was so unlike the Florida I expected. There were no grand tourist hotels. It was a peaceful small town very much like a New England town but with palms and tropical flowers. It had the sea and it had the writers and it had the pleasant atmosphere of being a wonderful place to work.

I've been able to set parts of stories here. In my novel, *The Truth about Lorin Jones*, part of the story takes place in Key West, which of course could never have happened if I hadn't been here. There's a story set in Key West in my collection of ghost stories, which is called *Women and Ghosts*. My novel *The Last Resort* also takes place in Key West and describes the local scene.

JOHN D. MACDONALD

We first came down here in September, 1949. My first impressions—clean, bright, windswept, relaxing. We poked around and we bought a place on Siesta Key. We lived on Point Crisp Road for eighteen years. Then we moved here. We built this house. It was started in 1968 and we moved into it in 1969 and we've been here ever since. But I don't think it's good for a writer to stay locked into one place if

*When did you first
come to Florida?*

*What were your first
impressions?*

*What aspects of your
work have been
affected as a result of
your time in the state?*

he can help it, because you've got to have some kind of input and I think geography helps a lot. So we have a little camp in the Adirondacks that we built in 1952. We have sort of an apartment thing, one story, in Acumal, which is about sixty miles below Cancun in Yucatan. In addition to that, we try to take a boat trip every year.

Florida is a good place for a home base. It is a little on the tacky side, it's a little bit second-class, really. Mostly because the political system in Florida has tended to make good government and good management impossible. We've had the county commissioner system in Florida for many, many years. If there was ever a system that was designed to enrich further the real estate dealers, and the lawyers, and the accountants, and the bankers—I can't think of it. The thing that makes Florida second-class is the little phrase: zoning exception. What good is zoning if everybody knows that you can get an exception, if you go to the right people.

I have used a Florida background and ambience in a few dozen novels.

What are my suggestions for the Governor of Florida?:

1. Make a strong move to change your cabinet officers from elective to appointive. It won't help any, but it will make future governors something more than stuffed owls sitting at the end of the table.

2. Move toward a state income tax plus a large and realistic impact fee on all new residential construction. Eight hundred new residents a day gravely endanger the infrastructure. We sag further and further behind in schools, roads, bridges, health care and all other essential services. With our climate, with too much advertising and promotion, and with no income tax and with inadequate impact fees, the whole eastern half of the country is like a huge funnel dripping people into this tiny peninsula.

THOMAS MCGUANE

I first came to Florida in 1948. My impressions were all of birds and lizards and land crabs. This was Boca Raton which seemed like the South Seas, as in Robert Louis Stephenson.

I have used the Keys as a setting for *Ninety-Two in the Shade*, *The Bushwacked Piano*, and *Panama*. My years in Florida affected my work primarily, in my view of Americans as an easily uprooted people.

ROLLIE MCKENNA

I visited Florida when I was a child. My grandparents, on my mother's side, started their fourth inn in Ft. Walton when the highway had just been opened up. I was going to Gulf Park College in Gulfport, Mississippi, at the time. That was my first encounter. I made many trips down here after that, to various places.

Professionally, my first association with Florida was in the '60s when I was working for this information agency doing pictures for a magazine called *America*, which was an inter-change propaganda magazine with the Russians. It had a *Life* magazine format. I came to Florida on assignment from them chiefly to photograph lower to middle income people who had retired to Florida, in St. Petersburg mainly. It was a wonderful assignment. The casual view is that you reach that age of retirement and you and your husband, if he's still alive, would go and you'd all sit around and twiddle your thumbs until you die which is absolutely the opposite of what I'd found. People were having a lot of fun. There were organized activities. They appeared to be enjoying life. Their grandchildren would come to visit. They were happy.

WILLIAM MANCHESTER

We had for several years, gone to the Caribbean each winter. We came to Long Boat Key in 1975 to visit some friends. We began coming down every year and bought this place about 1978. If you first came to Bradenton you'd have a dif-

*When did you first
come to Florida?*

*What were your first
impressions?*

*What aspects of your
work have been
affected as a result of
your time in the state?*

ferent impression than first coming to Long Boat Key. Long Boat Key's impressions are excellent. This area has a very strict law against commercial advertising and signs. If you cross the bridge into the next community you'll find all kinds of signs. But you can't do that here. The scenery, the water, and the people are very pleasant and low key.

I've never written about Florida. My work habits were formed when I was young. My hours are fewer here, but that comes with age. On a good day, I can turn out about 900 words, but that doesn't mean they all are printable.

I do a lot of thinking while I'm down here. I wonder what's going to happen with the arrival of complex technology. And this talk, well, it's more than just talk, of books which are not on paper, but which are on tape. Communication is in the throes of such a revolution. I wonder what's going to happen to another generation? Are people still going to read books as we did? A century ago that was the only way we could communicate. And then we had radio and motion pictures and television. I'm not even comfortable with the thoughts of the future. I've had a good life. I wouldn't want to live it over again. I wouldn't want to start again. I just don't think I'd be so lucky next time.

CONRAD MARCA-RELLI

We first came to Sarasota in the early '60's, and then we returned about 1980. In 1983, I built this house in Siesta Key that we enjoy very much. My studio is on the first floor, which is handy. I came back to Florida because it works for me. What attracts me here is the light and really, a feeling of utter freedom.

Artists seem to have a very special eye for places. They always seem to choose places that are pretty good because no matter where it is in Europe or here, the artists usually are the first ones to discover a place. Then in no time at all, the whole thing changes because too many people come. The public always has excelled in that. They've always found the right places like East Hampton, outside of New York, and all the other places in France that were discovered by artists.

JAMES MERRILL

As a baby. My four grandparents and both my parents were Floridians. My mother would have brought me to Jacksonville, her birthplace, before I was a year old. My impressions would have included her old black nurse, Jane Reid; my godparents, Mr. and Mrs. Blaid Burwell, and *their* baby, a daughter just my age; a steep staircase of gleaming wood in my grandmother's house; the taste of grits; and the lovely, joyous sounds of Southern women talking.

I like writing poems about places, and over the years have set perhaps six or eight of mine in Florida.

JAMES A. MICHENER

I don't recall the exact date I first visited Florida. That happened some time ago. But this time, I came toward the end of 1987. I had worked in Florida at Juno Beach, up by Palm Beach, and I had liked it there very much. I had seen most of Florida, east coast and west coast, just as a tourist. I wrote two of my books in Florida—the book on NASA and also, the book on Poland. So this is the third book I will have written in Florida.

I think if one is going to write about the Caribbean, he ought to live either on some island like Barbados, or in some Spanish center like Cartejena, or in Miami, which is the ipso-facto capitol of the Caribbean at the moment. You've got three choices. I would be perfectly happy in any one of them. Miami however, offers quite a few opportunities. It is the center of the tourist trade, it has a good airport and it has a good newspaper. On balance, it's probably a little better to work in Miami than it would be in Barbados or Cartejena. It's a good city and a good setting.

I reside in Florida. This is where I work. We pay our taxes in Pennsylvania, but I haven't been there in fifteen years. I live where I work.

*When did you first
come to Florida?*

*What were your first
impressions?*

*What aspects of your
work have been
affected as a result of
your time in the state?*

JULES OLITSKI

In 1976. It was by chance. I would usually go to New York in the winter. Early fall would come and it was time to leave New Hampshire and get to my studio in New York. But then I thought, I don't need to go to New York. I can paint any-where.

We came to Islamorada as guests of the owner of the Cheeca Lodge. It was extraordinary, the feeling of walking into the light. We would go fishing every day. I thought this was pretty exciting. So we went and rented the old Gentry house on the bay. I'd be here and Kristina would come out on weekends. I went across the street one day to a realtor. They took me to this house. Before I even got in the house, I said, I'll buy it. And I did. I found a dog out on the road and brought it home. That's how I got Molly, our great wonderful dog. I called Kris and said, "We bought a house. We got a dog." It turned out to be just the right house and the right dog.

My first impressions were of the sea and the sky, the great breathtaking beauty of it all, and the heart-thumping excitement that goes with Keys fishing.

I think painting is an internal vision that you carry about wherever you go. You don't necessarily change when you go from New Hampshire to New York, to Paris, or to the Florida Keys. But here, you feel as though you are always close to something divine, and that is what art is about—expressing that feeling. I would have trouble isolating a part of my painting and saying, here, this is the influence, but I know that the influence is there.

LARRY POONS

I first came for the motorcycle race at Daytona about 1969. I don't remember my first impression—maybe the heat. Then I was giving a talk in Ft. Lauderdale, by invitation, and a friend of ours suggested we come down to the Keys, and we did. That was about 1973 or '74. We made some friends right away. We liked the fishing. We felt at home and it was a nice place to get away to.

I don't know for sure if my work has been affected by my time here—there's no way for me to pinpoint that.

PADGETT POWELL

I was born in Gainesville, 1952. Moved all around. In Indian Head Acres, in Tallahassee, I could find arrowheads in the dirt path beneath our clothesline. In Ocoee, 2nd grade, some kids had no shoes, and a benefactor of mine who protected me from marble thugs came to school with his big toe held on by a piece of skin. His name was Lamar. His sister was tall and manly, and shot a good marble. She wore short-shorts. She and Lamar pooled their winnings—their marbles filled a 2-foot-square box.

ROBERT RAUSCHENBERG

I've had this property since 1963. At that time, the entire island was a jungle of palms and palmettos.

The work that has been affected by my being in Florida are the ones I've done here.

LARRY RIVERS

I came here first because I thought I had drug problems—like I was taking too many drugs. Actually, I'm exaggerating like mad. I came down here to get away from New York. That was fairly early, maybe 1946. I stayed for a little while. It was a completely different place at that time. I was playing my saxophone, although I didn't get jobs. I considered myself more of a musician at that time. This was South Beach and I think it was 5th Street and Collins. There were a lot of old Jewish people in the hotel there. It was a little off-putting because I had no way of relating to them. I don't mean the Jewish part at all because I'm a Jew. The thing was the age difference, and I was a musician, and I smoked pot, and

*When did you first
come to Florida?*

*What were your first
impressions?*

*What aspects of your
work have been
affected as a result of
your time in the state?*

these people had different concerns. I didn't identify with them at all, but it looked pretty and I was on the beach.

I did a painting from the 11th Street diner this year—kind of a Deco diner. This self-portrait is now, but I don't think of it as Miami, although it's done here. It may be called Larry on Ocean Drive, I'm not sure. I'm working from the photo someone took of me. I saw a very big painting of mine up in the Palm Beach area last night. I saw it and thought, "My God, I haven't made a painting that size in a long time." It inspired me to perhaps make a big painting when I get back to New York—just *big*. So you see, artists don't particularly work out of subjects or something. What it will be, I don't know, but I know I want to do a *big* painting.

JAMES ROSENQUIST

I came to Florida in 1953. I hitchhiked to see the motorcycle races in Daytona Beach. Florida was very rural then and oranges fell down on old Highway 1. I took a bus from Daytona to Key West. I did watercolors of the palmettos, waterfronts, and black shanty towns. Then I took an old C-46 and flew to Cuba for $26 roundtrip.

I didn't come back down until 1971 when I was invited by Don Saff to make prints at the Graphicstudio in Tampa. At that time, I was still living in New York. I returned in '74 to make more prints, and in 1976, I built this house on 28 acres right on the Gulf of Mexico. This is home. I do all my paintings here. You paint with a full eighty-eight Keys here. I can mix gorgeous colors in this light. I can mix sky-blue pinks. I can make orange-greens and violets. In New York it's all very, very dark. You can't see anything. It's like working in a dark tunnel.

BOB SHACOCHIS

I first came to Florida in the summer of 1969. I was seventeen years old. My first impression—flat, where a curve in the road was a nostalgic event. We moved to Tallahassee from the Outer Banks of North Carolina in 1988. Catfish announced that she wanted to go to law school in 1987. I said *Hooray*! Then she passed her LSATs and applied to various schools. Her criteria for applying to schools was climate. So we came here broke, sixty bucks in our pocket. We camped out in the backyard of a writer friend named Ben Green for a couple of weeks. The thing that got us in a house was the *GQ* column.

Florida does not cherish its literary resources very well. This baffles me. They focus on three or four writers, and that's it. Florida is brimming with talent. I know this sounds self-aggrandizing, but it's not, it's just to illustrate the point. I'm well known everywhere else in the country, but in Florida—and especially in Tallahassee. I can't even get invited to the Writer's Tea in Tallahassee. Whereas, I get invited to read at Lincoln Center with Joyce Carol Oates, and on Broadway with Geraldine Page, when she was alive. The state of Florida is not going to be considered a sophisticated state until it values its cultural treasures—not just its dead ones, or its easiest ones, but the whole spectrum. There's a hell of a lot *more* talent in Florida that goes unsung, but only in Florida. The rest of the country knows about them. Culturally, the difference between a California and a Florida is enormous—and I don't get it!

WILFRID SHEED

When I was seventeen, and that would have been in 1948. As I remember, I went to a meeting in a large park in Dade County where there was a debate going on between George Smathers and Claude Pepper. It was all about Truman's stand on civil rights. Both of these men were trying to find a formula to say they understood Southern tradition and the plight of the Negro. It was a glorious time in the sense that people had been moved, but it wasn't possible to say it yet.

I remember being fascinated by roads with houses, but without sidewalks and pedestrians. This gave me a sense of the American outback, which Miami certainly isn't anymore. Florida has always had that sense to me of an adventurous, last-resort kind of place, and Key West, of course, definitely so.

I didn't come back until we began to come to Sarasota. I would slip up to Bradenton to watch the Pittsburgh Pirates spring training.

ISAAC BASHEVIS SINGER

We had taken the train from New York to Miami in 1948, in the winter. When we came over the causeway in the taxi, I could hardly believe my eyes—the water, the buildings, the indescribable glow, and the palm trees. The palm trees especially made an impression on me. We stayed at the Hotel Pierre for eight dollars a day. We were young and we had little money and that seemed a bit much, but we got a room that had a balcony. I stood on that balcony and stared at a palm tree for hours and I was happy. When I came here for the first time, I had a feeling I had come to paradise.

It was at the Pierre and later, at the Crown Hotel that I wrote chapters of *The Family Moskat*, my first big novel. I have also published four stories which use Miami Beach as a setting—*Alone*, *Old Love*, *The Hotel*, and *A Party in Miami Beach*, which is the most humorous one and is closest to how I feel about Miami Beach, which is where we've lived since 1973.

PATRICK D. SMITH

My first visit to Florida was in 1933 at age six when my family came to Florida on a three week vacation trip—all the way down the west coast to Miami and then up the east coast. Back then it was a tropical wilderness except for the cities. From 1948 to 1966, I made at least two trips each year to Florida. I moved to Florida permanently in 1966. Needless to say, over the years since 1933, I have seen many changes in Florida and its way of life over a half century ago.

Since moving to Florida, I have written extensively about what has happened and is happening to nature in Florida, and the tragic results of so-called "progress." I have also written about the plight of the Seminole Indians and migrant workers.

SYD SOLOMON

I arrived in Sarasota after a big New Year's eve party early on the first day of 1946. I admired the landscape and the sleepy town atmosphere that was very much like Monterey, California. The idea that such a small town would have a museum of such major proportions and major collections was very exciting, and still is.

When I begin a painting I am usually thinking of one particular natural phenomenon, or particular place. Frequently it's reminiscent of some atmospheric condition, some chromatic intensity, an impression I have of the environment. The flatness of Sarasota's landscape has brought me to solicit strong diagonals and ascending compositions from the remarkable thunderheads and storm clouds that swell over the sea.

ROBERT STONE

I think I was first in Florida when I was on my way to New Orleans. I was hitchhiking and for whatever reason, I came by way of Jacksonville and then west, on 90. I was going back to New Orleans from New York. I must have gotten a ride that took me to Jacksonville, then I hitchhiked west. That probably would have been around 1960 or '61. North Florida in those days was much more Southern and less cosmopolitan, more intensely regional than it is now. It was like the Deep South. The first time I spent any time in South Florida, I came to get out on a shrimp boat. I wanted to put a shrimp boat in this novel, *A Flag for Sunrise*. I finally did get out on a boat and spent a couple of days out shrimping. That would have been in the early '70s. That was in Key West before the boats moved to Stock Island—when they were still in town. I don't remember the name of the captain, but I do remember the name of the boat—it was *The Water Brothers*.

I'm kind of interested in the Orlando area. What it was like around the time when Disney World was first being built. And also, in some of the history of that

When did you first come to Florida?

What were your first impressions?

What aspects of your work have been affected as a result of your time in the state?

area during the Seminole Wars. Although I haven't really written about that, it's something I'd like to get into.

PETER TAYLOR

We came to Key West in 1973 and stayed at the Pier House. My wife and I have many old friends here at just the same time we are.

We bought a house here in 1976. Eleanor and I would come down after Christmas and stay until the beginning of April. Key West is where I was able to do my real writing, when I was away from the university. We like Charlottesville a lot, but I don't get much work done there. Teaching pretty much fills my time.

After we sold the Key West house we bought a house in Gainesville and began to spend the coldest months there. My wife's sister and brother-in-law, the poet Don Justice, along with other friends of ours, were living there at the time. We like that environment as well. And we enjoy the quaint neighboring towns. In Key West, we had palm trees and tropical plants, in Gainesville we have moss and ferns and big beautiful live oak trees. But I manage to keep coming back to Key West. As a matter of fact, I have been looking for another house down there.

JERRY N. UELSMANN

In 1960. I've always felt there are places where you are born and places where you were supposed to have been born. I happened to have been born in inner-city Detroit. I feel I should have been born in the South. I think my work relates to a sort of gothic tradition that exists in the South. It exists in literary forms and I can relate very much to that. I now consider myself a Southerner.

I think North Florida is a wonderful undiscovered part of America. It has these live oak trees and springs and swamps and vines. It has always been very engaging to me and it's a very difficult environment to photograph. There is a sense of mystery that occurs within that environment.

RICHARD WILBUR

Most of my experience of Florida has been Key West, which I first visited in the mid-60s. It proved to be, as a friend has told me, "a mixture of beauty and tackiness." I liked the amiable poverty of Key West of some years ago; I liked its being in many ways a backwater; I was delighted by its tolerant diversity. There is much to be said for the subsequent restorations and renovations, but I detest the condominiums which have sprung up along the shores, and feel that Key West has acquired its boutiques and fancy restaurants at a certain cost in character.

Key West has proved to be a good place to work and to relax from work. It took me many years to possess and internalize a place so different from my New England, but at last I have celebrated the island in a few poems like "Bone Key," "Fabrications," and "Security Lights, Key West."

CHARLES WILLEFORD

In 1953, from Los Angeles. I remember it being ungodly hot. That was one of my first impressions, although these summers still get to me. Of course it was a lot different back in '53 than it is today. Things were a little easier going and people were poor down here then. I was living in West Palm Beach for the first seven years. It was losing population every year, not gaining. Every year it was losing two to five thousand people. Then the air base left. Those people just moved out and left their houses empty and didn't make any payments. The houses became vandalized. It looked like a ghost town there for a couple of years. People forget about that. Downtown West Palm Beach has never recovered.

A writer reflects the environment he lives in. The one that he knows, sees, and watches. This is a dynamic city. There's a lot going on here. I can't think of a better city for a writer to be in. There are a million stories here that haven't been tapped. It's got a lot of money, it's got the poorest people, the richest people, and it's booming.

When did you first come to Florida?

What were your first impressions?

What aspects of your work have been affected as a result of your time in the state?

I had to make up my own police department. Mine is much better than the one we have here in Miami. The police department is so corrupt. If I tried to write about it the way it really was—people wouldn't believe it. One out of ten is under suspension, there are nine cops being tried for home invasion. You can't write about that because people wouldn't believe it.

JOY WILLIAMS

My father won a free trip to Daytona Beach in a supermarket drawing in Portland, Maine. I was ten. We drove down in our Buick Century. I got a terrific sunburn—absolutely immobilizing. We were in Florida for five days and I never saw anything. My eyes swelled completely shut. I was sure the experience would be fatal. Florida is fatal, I thought.

Many of my essays are very much concerned with Florida and her trampled beauty.

What are my suggestions for the governor of Florida? Preserve wild lands, use the tourist tax on lodging to acquire open space and clean up the environment. Everybody knows Florida's here. You don't have to introduce her further.

2
CONVERSATIONS

*Where do you
work best?*

EDWARD ALBEE

In my head. I used to write on ocean liners, but they've taken those away from me so I can't do that very much anymore. Wherever I am—I write more in my head than on the page. I think about a play a long time before I put it down. The actual writing takes a fairly brief amount of time. I can work on airplanes, walking, sitting somewhere—it doesn't matter much.

RICHARD ANUSZKIEWICZ

I do my work in my studio in Englewood, New Jersey.

ANN BEATTIE

Place is important in terms of my level of happiness and that, of course, feeds into everything that I am—writer among those things. Every place has its advantages and its problems. But one thing to say about Key West is the obvious, which is that there are a lot of writers here. Ultimately, they would like you to play with them. But if you can't play with them because you have to work—they really do understand that.

JOHN MALCOLM BRINNIN

Not on unpopulated islands or on the slopes of barren mountains, both of which I've tried, but in any place where the essential factor is a lot of activity I can ignore. On shipboard, for instance, in Key West, or Venice.

PHILIP BURTON

I work best in my study surrounded by books. I've written two books in Key West. Oh yes, I'm hopeless at any machine. I'm a two-finger typist. I have a look at the keys and I don't know what's happening on the paper. It's agony—*agony* for me to type. But I do manage it somehow. Then I get someone to make a good copy of my mess.

PHILIP CAPUTO

In my head. My surroundings sometimes play a role in getting the juices to flow, but once they start flowing, I could write in Grand Central Station, or in an airplane, or in a disco. Indeed, I have, on occasion.

JOHN CHAMBERLAIN

It doesn't matter—wherever I've got some scrap lying around.

JOHN CIARDI

In Metuchen and here in Key West. In either place, I seem to spend day after day at my desk. I get up, start out with a cup of coffee and the next thing I know Judith is in the study asking me if I mean to go through supper still in pajamas. I'm thinking seriously of spending six months without writing a word.

HARRY CREWS

At home in Gainesville. I usually start at 4:00 A.M. and work until 9:30. Then I go to the gym, come back and work in the afternoons—yesterday afternoon until 2:00 this morning, but if I don't get something going by 9:30, then the day is shot, in terms of writing.

Where do you work best?

I start by writing in longhand, in this big chair in my living room, or lying on the floor or in bed, or sitting on a park bench. Then I type that, editing as I go, on this manual typewriter that's older than I am. Everything I've ever written was written on this typewriter made in 1926. The next thing is to put whatever it is that I'm working on at the time in this word processing machine. That's so I can see the words and move them around better than I could if I were cutting and pasting. The word processor is a great thing, but it's bad for writers because it speeds things up. Most writers, myself included, need to slow down. Writing is a slow process and I'll be the first to say I don't need things accelerating or happening any faster than they already are.

ANNIE DILLARD

It doesn't matter. Once you're well underway on a work—you can work anywhere.

MARJORY STONEMAN DOUGLAS

At home in my small house in Coconut Grove, which is more of a workshop than a residence.

RICHARD EBERHART

I guess at night, in my study at my home in Hanover, New Hampshire. I am not a poet who can write at a certain time of the day or night. Some people can, I'm sporadic. I couldn't sit down every day at a certain hour. A poem might come to me at any time of the day or night, and I might jot it down. It might be good or it might not.

DICK FRANCIS

Nowadays, I work best here in Florida, sitting on the balcony looking out to sea—getting ideas. The best thing about being a writer is not the writing, it's doing the research and learning about new things. We travel all over the world doing this sort of thing. We've been to Australia; we've been to Moscow; we've been to Italy, Norway, New Zealand, Hawaii, Canada. I said to my publisher about ten years ago, "Will you publish a book of mine which isn't about racing, or horses?" She sat for awhile—she said, "Yes, we'll publish anything you write. We'd rather you didn't write one though, your readers would be disappointed." So I've never wandered away from the four-legged animals.

MARILYN FRENCH

Florida, most years. In New York there are so many distractions. I do work well here—the sun, the ocean—looking out at the blue skies and greenness really cheers me up. If I get stuck, I can go down and take a long walk on the beach and have my characters argue with each other. Or, if I'm writing discursive prose—argue with myself, and come back and be ready to start again. I don't get up in the mornings, I get up in the middle of the day. I work 'til maybe two in the morning—go to sleep about four or five.

DUANE HANSON

Any place that has sufficient light and space.

JOHN HERSEY

I made the unhappy discovery in about 1951 or 1952 that I could work any-where. Before that, I'd had the comfortable feeling that I had to be at my desk. I had to line the pencils up in a certain way and follow that ritual in my study. But, that year, I had to do some traveling and I found I could write in railroad trains,

Where do you
work best?

hotels, and so on. Actually, now, I'm happiest writing in two rooms—one here in Key West and one on Martha's Vineyard. Here, I look out at this marvelous foliage we have; there, I look out at the sea and watch the boats go by. I'm very happy in both places.

CARL HIAASEN

While I can write in a busy, chaotic newsroom, I'm sure I write *better* in the quiet of my office (which, by the way, has no view of the water. I've got enough distractions).

EVAN HUNTER

Anywhere.

DONALD JUSTICE

Probably here in my study or else, when I'm out walking.

WILLIAM KING

Anywhere, it doesn't matter. That depends on available materials. I've pretty much arranged my life for the benefit of the sculptures, for better or for worse.

JAMES KIRKWOOD

I can work almost anywhere if given a room to myself and some peace and quiet. I do tend to work best in Key West for many reasons: I'm away from New York and Hollywood, so the phones are not constantly ringing. I'm not seduced into an active social life all that much. There is something about the air in Key West that is magical and conducive to writing. Something chemical about the place itself. I work best there in the early morning to noon.

JOHN KNOWLES

I've worked everywhere. I've worked in the South of France at the height of the tourist season. I can work in the middle of New York City. I can work in the woods of Long Island where I had a house for twenty years—in a little backwater near Southampton. I work well here in Florida.

ELMORE LEONARD

I work best in Birmingham, Michigan, at home in my study. I compose in longhand. I'll do anywhere from a page to several pages in longhand crossing out as I go along. Then I'll put that on my typewriter. My typewriter is a regular 1972 Olympia, office model, not electric and it's getting hard to find ribbons for it. I'm trying to make that typewriter last. I'm definitely not going into the computer, word processor business. That just doesn't appeal to me. I write in longhand because to me, that's writing.

ROY LICHTENSTEIN

I work best in my New York studio. I don't tend to work away from the studio, or outside, or while traveling, or any of those things. I may make some drawings, which probably have nothing to do with the place I'm at. I tend to paint in my studio.

The number of things I do a year vary tremendously. Part of that is the size or the complexity of a painting. I think I've been productive all the way along. Actually, I have a sort of dread of not being productive.

*Where do you
work best?*

ROBERT LUDLUM

Pretty much anywhere. I write by longhand. I send my material up to my secretary in Connecticut from wherever I am and she puts it into one of those word processing computers. I'm so frightened of it I won't walk into the office. I work both in Florida and in Connecticut or, in planes or in trains.

ALISON LURIE

I work best where it is quiet and I do not have to struggle against the weather. For this reason, Key West in the wintertime is ideal.

JOHN D. MACDONALD

Probably at our camp on Piseco Lake in the Adirondaks, but only because there are fewer interruptions and distractions there than in Sarasota.

THOMAS MCGUANE

It doesn't matter.

ROLLIE MCKENNA

Wherever there's sufficient light, and if it involves photographing people—in pleasant surroundings with someone not too stand-offish or stiff, which then allows the opportunity for leisurely picture taking.

WILLIAM MANCHESTER

For me it's not so much a matter of where, it's *when*. There are a great many writers who write well in the morning. Paul Horgan is a friend of mine and by noon, his day is done. John Hersey was that way, and he sailed in the afternoons. But I've never been able to work in the morning. I write in the afternoon or in the evening. In the morning I just fool around and get ready to write. I can organize notes, but don't put words on paper. I've had to make a number of adjustments with the arrival of technology and the word processor. I think well with a fountain pen in my hand. It's hard for me to write directly on a typewriter or on a computer screen. There's a magic in transforming thoughts into words on a page. It's mysterious and I don't think it should be examined too closely. If it works, leave it alone.

CONRAD MARCA-RELLI

If I work in any way it's in reaction to a place, not an acceptance of it. For instance, if it's a very quiet place—out of boredom, I might work more. I might get involved in problems that are much more difficult to solve because I have all the time in the world to give it to them. So in that way, a place contributes to me. I would say that the only way that the light affects me is like it's done in Spain. When the light is very sharp I paint with less color and go into more black and white. I've had a very somber palette for a long time and possibly it's due to that.

JAMES MERRILL

In places—like Stonington, Connecticut (my home for over thirty years), or a house I once had in Greece, or Key West—that have grown familiar enough to work in. Once I know them, as it were, by heart, I can pursue my own thoughts in their midst, undistracted by their original charm or strangeness.

*Where do you
work best?*

JAMES A. MICHENER

I have worked in almost every climate and every area in the world. I worked very well in Indonesia in a pair of shorts, tremendous perspiration, the temperature around 95 and the humidity around 97. I also worked very well in Northern Alaska—in the land of perpetual night. I really don't have any preconception about writing. I just need a big desk and a quiet space. I don't need a good landscape or anything like that. I just need a work space.

I think for many men the most productive period begins around the age of forty-five or forty-six, when you've got things sorted out. You realize the rest of the run is a finite thing. That everybody you've met so far over the age of ninety, ultimately dies. So you rather assume that you will, and I think that's a pretty good assumption. You are more relaxed—you're with it. Whatever powers you have, have matured. I think that's the great working period.

JULES OLITSKI

At this time, I work best in my studio in the Florida Keys and my studio on an island in a lake in New Hampshire.

I work at night. This is a habit left over from my childhood. It is the time when my family was asleep and I could wander through the house reading and thinking. It was the only time I could be myself and it is a habit so deeply ingrained in me that I have never changed.

LARRY POONS

Wherever I'm working.

PADGETT POWELL

University lunchrooms.

ROBERT RAUSCHENBERG

Wherever I am. I've worked in China, I've worked in the Ghandi Ashauin in India, I've worked in hotel rooms. I'm sensitive to the environment and the place, but so far I haven't found a place that is abortive to creative thinking.

LARRY RIVERS

South Hampton, but I do paintings almost everywhere I go.

JAMES ROSENQUIST

In Florida—because of the light.

BOB SHACOCHIS

Home—where I never am. Working, you just have to shed everything away and focus. I work at night because I still seem to be on some kind of college exam program. The phone doesn't ring and I'm free to concentrate. I begin after I walk the dogs around 10:00 P.M., until 2:00 or 3:00 A.M.—last night it was 4:30.

WILFRID SHEED

I like plenty of light when I'm working and that is absolutely the only require-ment. I actually tried to work with two small children scratching at the door and that sort of knocked the stuffing out of me as far as having a favorite place to write. In fact, some of the best stuff I did was in a Volkswagen bus that we once owned where they couldn't get at me. I would lock the doors and make faces at them and eventually they'd go away. After that, I thought just give me a room which isn't too noisy. To get started, I like it to be quiet and I like plenty of light. And *that*, I would fight for.

*Where do you
work best?*

ISAAC BASHEVIS SINGER

In Miami Beach where I work everyday. I have a small desk in the bedroom that has good light and I write with a Yiddish typewriter, but it's getting more difficult to locate parts when it needs repairs.

PATRICK D. SMITH

I can work anywhere, from a dining room table to whatever is handy. I do most of my work at home. A writer has to accept any work atmosphere, wherever it is.

SYD SOLOMON

I wish I knew.

ROBERT STONE

I think I've got a lot of good work done up in Connecticut. Maybe I work best up there—up on Long Island Sound in West Port. I really have tried to work on the move. I think the place is less important than the immediate circumstances. I like to work in the morning. I like to really start the day that way. I think my requirements for being able to work are fairly simple—I just need some peace and quiet and the access to my thoughts. Other than that, I think I can do it on the run. Especially as the technology gets very simple and the machines are more and more portable. I work with a word processor.

PETER TAYLOR

Mornings are my writing time, regardless of where I am. But I'm to the point now where I can write anywhere. It's almost like a lady's knitting, I always have it with me. All I need is a pad of paper. I always write with a pencil and I don't cross out lines. I erase sometimes half a page at a time.

JERRY N. UELSMANN

In the early part of my career I did a lot of photography almost exclusively in North Florida and some down on the beaches in Sarasota. Now that I have the opportunity to travel, I photograph everywhere. But the main work for me occurs in the darkroom. Essentially, I'm an introvert. The work I do occurs primarily when I'm alone, but I'm comfortable with that. For me, the creative moment occurs in the darkroom.

RICHARD WILBUR

I work best in a simple room with a good light and no telephone. I like to have a good, small reference library at hand. A comfortable armchair. A supply of #2 soft pencils. The view from the window should not be too distractingly busy or vast.

CHARLES WILLEFORD

I can work just about anywhere. As long as you do your work everyday, you'll get something—eventually. I write in the mornings about two or three hours a day and try to turn out about a thousand words a day.

JOY WILLIAMS

In a room with no view.

CONVERSATIONS 3

What do you think you'd have done had you not become an artist or writer ?

EDWARD ALBEE

I can't conceive of a life other than the one I'm living.

RICHARD ANUSZKIEWICZ

I don't know.

ANN BEATTIE

I think writing is the only imaginative thing I'm aware of that I can do. I suppose my only other skills, and they're certainly not extraordinary, are organizational skills. I really would imagine that since I didn't have any career plans, you might have found me as somebody's executive secretary.

JOHN MALCOLM BRINNIN

That of a cultural archeologist.

PHILIP BURTON

I really am a born teacher. I was never trained as a teacher, but that's what I would have been—that's what I am I suppose.

PHILIP CAPUTO

I have no idea what I'd be doing, though I do know what I would like to have been: a test pilot for high-performance aircraft.

JOHN CHAMBERLAIN

A saloon keeper if I had stuck with the family tradition. I think we had about six generations of saloon keepers. Otherwise, probably an aeronautical engineer.

JOHN CIARDI

I had gone to college thinking I'd be a lawyer, but I got hooked on English courses and kept taking them until I became unemployable.

HARRY CREWS

Farming.

ANNIE DILLARD

A painter, I think, without question. Although I was all set to go get a Ph.D. in Theology too, but I was married and couldn't go on with my education at that point. If I hadn't been a writer, I'd have been a painter.

MARJORY STONEMAN DOUGLAS

I haven't the slightest idea and couldn't care less.

RICHARD EBERHART

When I got out of the war I became a businessman, but I was a writer on the side. I was always a doodleist. No matter what I was doing in the outside world there was always this compulsion to write something down. So I suppose I would have become and still have been a businessman. Maybe that's why I had such a good friendship with Wallace Stevens.

What do you think you'd have done had you not become an artist or writer ?

DICK FRANCIS

I suppose I might have been a race course official in some way such as a starter, or a judge, or a steward or trainer.

MARILYN FRENCH

I have often wished I could have many lives. I'd love to be an archaeologist. I'd love to be a photographer—a character in one of my novels is a photographer, but I don't have a good eye. I don't think I could make it as a photographer. I'd like to be a painter. I wish I could have been a singer. I'd love to be a dancer. I like things in the arts and I would like something in which you could use your whole self—your body, your voice, your sense of music, your sense of the visual— all of that. It would be wonderful. An actress I guess; I would like to be an actress.

DUANE HANSON

I'm afraid I'd be out of work.

JOHN HERSEY

I think I probably would have wound up in some second-rate orchestra some-where playing one of the second violin stands.

CARL HIAASEN

Teaching.

EVAN HUNTER

I can't possibly imagine being anything but a writer.

DONALD JUSTICE

I would like to have been a musician, that would have been my preference. Otherwise, I probably would have settled down to teaching literature in a college. I have always liked literature from early childhood on. So that would also have been a happy solution for me.

WILLIAM KING

I'd either be dead, which is probable, or I'd be an underpaid alcoholic draftsman in an architect's office.

JAMES KIRKWOOD

I would probably still be an actor, although by this time I might well be institutionalized. Translated that means—crazy. Why crazy? Because when an actor is out of work—that leads the way to madness. And if I were not an Olivier or a movie star constantly in demand I'd be out of work *a lot*. I thank God I found my way into writing.

JOHN KNOWLES

I think I'd be coaching and teaching swimming. I was a very good swimmer. I held a world record, although it was sort of a fluke. It was the mile relay record. I was on the varsity team at Yale and we broke the record which simply meant that we had great depth in our swimming team because eighteen people swim 1,750 yards. So seventeen swimmers swim 100 yards, and one swimmer swims 50—I was one of those swimmers.

*What do you think
you'd have done
had you not become
an artist or writer ?*

ELMORE LEONARD

I'd be writing something. I was with an advertising agency for ten years. In 1961 I left the agency where I was writing Chevrolet ads to go on my own to have more time to write. But we bought a house and suddenly I had to make a living. So that from '61 to '66 I did a lot of freelance writing on the side and didn't do any fiction writing at all. I would probably have been in advertising—that was a way to make a living.

ROY LICHTENSTEIN

I don't have the vaguest idea really, because I was leaning toward being an artist ever since I was fifteen, and that was a few years ago. But I think I might have been an inventor. If I were to guess—that's what I would say.

ROBERT LUDLUM

There is no question, I would be teaching at a university somewhere. I had already made up my mind to leave the theatre world. Actually, I had sent out my academic credentials and resumes to various universities and had two or three offer me a job based on my experiences as a producer, as well as in the humanities, fine arts and theatre arts—that is where I expected to be. I thought I'd be writing in a very minor way. At this point in my life, I thought I would be with any luck, a tenured professor somewhere.

ALISON LURIE

If I had not become a writer, I would probably have been a librarian, or an editor in a publishing house, at least for awhile, since those are the jobs I had before I began to publish and teach. At present, I would be retired.

JOHN D. MACDONALD

I would be retired from a career in industrial management or investment banking, where I used my Harvard Business School/Wharton School, Syracuse B.S. in Business Administration.

THOMAS MCGUANE

I would have practiced law or had a small factory in a small Midwestern town and ruled it with an iron hand.

ROLLIE MCKENNA

Who knows? I feel, in a way, that I was practically predestined to be a photographer. I grew up in a hotel room from the age of three to fifteen. I was exposed to all kinds of personalities so I was never really afraid of people. My grandfather was an architect, and was a very good artist, as well. I always had a leaning toward representational painting and drawing. So I really came to photography through the back door, in one sense. All the ingredients were there.

WILLIAM MANCHESTER

That's a tough one. Writing is really the only thing I know how to do. I might have become a teacher. It's hard for me to imagine myself without some writing skills because I've always had them. They have always been a source of pleasure.

CONRAD MARCA-RELLI

I'd have been a brain surgeon. I have always been interested in medicine. At this point, with all the commerciality and pretense we see in the art world, I wonder if it was a good idea for me to have lived my life as an artist.

What do you think you'd have done had you not become an artist or writer ?

JAMES MERRILL

Perhaps a chef or butler in a small household. I do that presently as a hobby, so I'll be ready, just in case.

JAMES A. MICHENER

I have regularly thought that had I not been a writer, I'm pretty sure I would have been a labor union organizer. I see that very clearly. That was the way bright young guys got ahead in those days when there were no other ways. I would have had some kind of normal job. I'm sure I would have gravitated toward union management and probably wound up something like Walter Reuther, or McDonald, or Able.

JULES OLITSKI

God knows.

LARRY POONS

I don't know.

PADGETT POWELL

Roofing.

ROBERT RAUSCHENBERG

I would probably be raising more dogs or working a nursery—that's a plant nursery. Truck driving is not too far off because then you still travel.

LARRY RIVERS

I'd be dead probably because if I had stuck to music, I probably would have ended up a total druggie, I think. But I got interested in painting. I didn't do it to save myself. To me, it was another activity with intellectual content. With painting you can tell a story—you can talk about the world a little more.

JAMES ROSENQUIST

I wanted to be an aviator, because my mother and father were aviators, or a cattle rancher.

BOB SHACOCHIS

Maybe a graphic designer for magazines. Maybe a commercial fisherman. I've worked as a carpenter. I could certainly be an editor. I'm just afraid if I didn't write, I wouldn't be an educated person.

WILFRID SHEED

I really don't think I would have persevered that well with anything else. Writing is the work I love and I don't know how I would fare with work I didn't love. My father took a law degree and my son has become a lawyer. I guess that is what else I would have become.

ISAAC BASHEVIS SINGER

I cannot imagine not writing.

What do you think you'd have done had you not become an artist or writer ?

PATRICK D. SMITH

Public relations.

SYD SOLOMON

I don't even want to know.

ROBERT STONE

I might have been a journalist. But if I hadn't been a writer of any kind, I don't know, it's hard to say. I probably would have done something to do with language. It's likely I would have been a journalist if I wasn't a writer of fiction.

PETER TAYLOR

Apart from teaching, I'm afraid I'd be hopeless at anything other than writing.

JERRY N. UELSMANN

I sometimes think if I were a singer, I'd be Jimmy Buffet. I love his songs and I can relate to the narrative. It's interesting because essentially, I am an introvert. The work I do occurs primarily when I'm alone. I spend a great deal of time alone, in the dark no less, but I'm very comfortable with that. I guess my fantasies of other lives involve a much more public persona. I like the idea that the graphic artist does have a low profile, unlike a performer. I would hate to face the pressure of having to get up in front of thousands of people. In essence I do some of that when I lecture, but it's not a comfortable way for me to be.

RICHARD WILBUR

I think I could be quite happy operating an herb farm, with one or two greenhouses.

CHARLES WILLEFORD

Probably a painter if I had stuck with it. I never did find exactly what I wanted to do as a painter. I kept changing. I was influenced by other work that I liked, then I'd realize—hell, that's not me. I never really developed my own style. I probably would have if I had stuck with it.

JOY WILLIAMS

If I was a tree what kind of tree would I like to be? Let me think about this one.

Conversations *4*

What is the best piece of advice you were ever given and, what piece of advice would you offer an aspiring artist/author?

EDWARD ALBEE

I think the best piece of advice I was ever given was given to me by Thornton Wilder—a great playwright by the way. His work is not admired as much as it should be. I gave him a lot of my poetry to read. He read it and he didn't like it very much. I was twenty-two or twenty-three and he said "I don't like this poetry very much, you ought to write plays."

The advice I would give to somebody who thinks he is a playwright: make absolutely certain that it is something that you have to do! Something without which you will be an incomplete person. And be prepared for a lot of heartbreak, a lot of weariness, a lot of the arbitrary. If it is something you just think would be interesting to do and make a buck at, don't do it, it's too tough a racket. But if it is something without which you would be incomplete, then jump in—you have to be yourself.

RICHARD ANUSZKIEWICZ

The best piece of advice I have ever received was when Josef Albers told me not to get sidetracked with such diversions as house renovation or construction, but to spend that valuable time on my own work.

My advice to aspiring young artists today would be, "If you don't make it in your twenties, be prepared for a long, hard struggle, and if you make it in your 20's, save your money."

ANN BEATTIE

I'm very good at filtering advice out. I think you have to be extremely autonomous as a writer. If advice does click with you, then I think that's wonderful. I have a lot invested in keeping those things out. I think people are filled with good intentions and even extremely wise things that they have said. In terms of being directly applied to my life, I fight against it—I've got a filtering system.

In terms of giving advice—the one thing that has occurred to me in recent years to remark upon is that I tell writers that it is a very private activity and you shouldn't feel at all that you, in effect, have to explain yourself. In other words, when you're doing the rough draft of something—if it seems crazy and out of your control, that really doesn't matter. It matters that you get it into shape before it's sent off for publication. It matters that you realize what you're grappling with and you try to come to terms with it. A lot of times, I've realized that with no bad intentions, people want me to say to them that even though my life on the surface might look very differently, actually we have a lot of similarities and I'm just like them. I really don't think I am. I'm not saying I'm better than them, I'm just saying that I really don't think my life is very similar to someone who works in an office. Without realizing it, I think you can become defensive as a writer. You can waste time by saying, oh—well, I work everyday. Yes, this is very serious to me. You see, I can prove that because I have a schedule. I've done this and I've done that. You don't have to say anything—the proof is in the pudding. I urge people not to talk much.

JOHN MALCOLM BRINNIN

Two pieces, equally depressing. a) Poets and novelists never finish the works they embark upon, but abandon them. b) The writer as artist never produces what he or she wants to write but what he or she deserves to write.

My advice to an aspiring writer is read, read, read. Today, more than ever before, writers aspiring to literature are prepared for nothing until they have read everything.

PHILIP BURTON

I'll tell you about actors first. I ran a school in New York, which is still doing very well, the American Musical and Dramatic Academy. When I took students in, I didn't want to see an audition, I wanted to see the motivation, first. If it was to

What is the best piece of advice you were ever given and, what piece of advice would you offer an aspiring artist/author?

see their name in lights—goodbye! If it was because they were happiest in acting then I would take them in for a semester. They were free to leave at the end of the semester, I was free to ask them to go. I knew what their work was like.

If your happiness is in acting, not in the acclaim you may get *if* you are a star, because not one in 50,000 is going to make that, then you stand a chance. Similarly for writers, if the desire to express yourself is the important thing, not being a great popular success and making a lot of money, if your joy is in the expression, if when you've finished the work there is a great sense of satisfaction rather than in selling it, then you stand a chance. Anybody who has his dream full of big lights and lots of money will be ill-advised to take any artistic career. The chances of his succeeding are very remote. There is no happiness like finishing the work, whether anybody else ever reads it or not. Then, he has a chance. Then he or she is rightly inspired.

PHILIP CAPUTO

Advice I was given: show, don't tell. When you are writing well, quit at the end of the day while you still have something to say so you won't have to face a blank page with a blank brain the next morning. Writing serious novels is lonely and full of pain and fear, and not to be entered into light-heartedly.

Advice I would give:

1. If you have the talent, you will eventually be published. The myth of the undiscovered genius is exactly that—a myth.

2. Talent without discipline is like a river without a course.

3. Do not expect to make a lot of money. If you do, continue to live as if you haven't. You never know when you'll need a few bucks to tide you over your dry periods. Do not, unless you earn enough to last three generations, think of yourself as rich.

4. Try to lead as quiet a life as possible, and save your energies for your work. If you marry, seek a mate who is emotionally stable and exceptionally under-

standing of those—like writers—who are not. Once you've found him or her, as the case may be, do not let him or her go for anything—or anyone.

5. If humanly possible, do not become a writer.

JOHN CHAMBERLAIN

Get a good paying job and watch your health.

JOHN CIARDI

The thing about would-be writers today is that they've been nursed into thinking that any belch is an attempt at self-expression and that any attempt must be rewarded. It seems not to have occurred to them that one may try and fail, or that they live among a people who really did their homework when they went to school.

As I once said to one of my students: "I, too, want the impromptu, but I find that it's what begins to happen at about the twentieth draft."

HARRY CREWS

Probably the best piece of advice I was ever given about writing was given to me by Andrew Lytle who said, "The middle of a thing is no place to judge it from." Everything you write—in the middle of it, it looks like it's not going to work. I've thought I can't finish this, or I don't know how this ends, or even if I do finish this it's going to be the most sophomoric, mawkish, bullshit thing anybody ever wrote. I've thought that with everything I've ever written. He always said just to suck it up and go ahead and finish the damn thing and at least give yourself a chance to fail legitimately. Nothing more is required of anybody but that they do the best they can. When you've given a thing your best shot you ought to go to bed and sleep well. Most of us don't because we don't like to fail. Primarily, I

What is the best
piece of advice you
were ever given and,
what piece of advice
would you offer an
aspiring artist/author?

think that failure almost inevitably results not from a lack of talent, or a lack of ability, but from a lack of will, or a lack of courage.

Advice to an aspiring writer—that's easy—write! Don't worry about going to New York or going to San Francisco or going any damn where. Put down your bucket where you are and write, and write, and write, and write. Writers are by definition, people who write. This has nothing to do with publishing, nothing to do with fame, praise, or money—it just has to do with writing. When somebody comes to me and says that they want to be a writer, I always want to know how much they've written today. Don't tell me how much you wrote yesterday, or how much you plan to write tomorrow, tell me how much you wrote *today*. And if the answer is nothing—well, then I'm inclined to think your chances are fairly poor.

ANNIE DILLARD

"Keep 'em guessing." (R. H. W. Dillard, my first husband)

Writers need to read what's been written.

MARJORY STONEMAN DOUGLAS

The best piece of advice I ever had was from a Latin teacher in high school—to make lasting friendships in college.

My advice to an aspiring writer is start writing!

RICHARD EBERHART

I guess I'd use the word persistence. It seems to me you have to *persist* to be an artist in America. You must never give up or give in. You must stand to your last. Persevere and let the chips fall where they may.

The Groundhog was written in twenty minutes and it has already lasted over half a century and is called a great poem. When I was writing it I had no idea that it was going to be a great poem. I was not aware really, that it was going to even be a good poem. I was *compelled* to write it. It was a profound expression of the totality of my being. It had to be said just the way it was.

DICK FRANCIS

To be accurate. Do your research. Get your facts right. Mary and I spend months of the year researching subjects and getting the facts right because when I'm reading a book and come across inaccuracies, it puts me off the book. I only once was criticized for an inaccuracy. In my second book I called the London School of Music, the London College of Music.

MARILYN FRENCH

I don't think I ever got any good advice. I think I always seemed to know exactly what I was about and what I was doing. People did not presume to give me advice although I probably could have used it.

I used to teach and I got very close to a lot of my students. We always had classes in my living room and I could hear what they expected from life. I used to say to them, "Just remember, you can have it all—but, not all at once." I think young people grow up expecting to have it all and expecting that it all comes together in one moment. So there is always the ache no matter what you have because you don't have something else. Just wait, if you really commit yourself to it, you will have it. You'll lose something else though. There's just not enough energy in us all to have it all at once. There is a piece of advice I would mention for young writers. I notice that a lot of young writers are really ignorant. They don't read. They think that you just pick up a pencil, or a typewriter, or word processor and you write. They don't have the grounding in the literature of the past that all writers of earlier generations had. I do think that young writers should read.

What is the best piece of advice you were ever given and, what piece of advice would you offer an aspiring artist/author?

DUANE HANSON

Carl Milles, the great Swedish sculptor who worked under Rodin, once said to me when I was a student in Cranbrook Academy of Art, "Do good work and you will be recognized." I thought he was simple-minded for saying that. But on June 3, 1986, I had a number of sculptures in his old studio in Stockholm. King Carl XVI Gustaf came to the opening and shook my hand.

JOHN HERSEY

My first job was working for Sinclair Lewis as his secretary and he quoted something to me that a very important teacher of his had said, "Genius is nine-tenths application of the seat of the pants to the seat of the chair," and that has always reverberated for me. My own advice to a young person who wants to write can be put in these words: read and write. I think the great writers are the best teachers and the only way to get anything done is to sit down and do it.

CARL HIAASEN

Keep writing, you can't get discouraged. Everything you do can be improved. There isn't a sentence I've ever written that couldn't have been a better sentence, or a character I've ever invented that couldn't have been better developed, or a plot that couldn't have been tighter or more clear. I've heard writers say, that's the best thing I've ever done. The writers I respect all look and say, when you think you can't do any better—throw the typewriter away.

EVAN HUNTER

Given today's publishing scene, I would advise an aspiring writer to give it up and develop a strong backhand instead. If he persists, I would advise him to write with his head and his heart, and to believe he is terrific no matter what anyone else tells him.

DONALD JUSTICE

I really can't remember any good advice I was ever given.

Old advice is still the good advice, like for a writer—write at the highest possible level you can manage. I think any writer profits from reading widely, but probably from following his or her own prescriptions in reading rather than anybody else's. You follow your own bent.

WILLIAM KING

Once you get started you are at the mercy of the process. Any advice would be to the business part of this—like lawyer advice, or doctor advice, or business manager advice, or dealer advice. Advice just gets in your way. Artists are artists and there isn't any such thing. There is encouragement or there is discouragement, I think.

My sculpture teacher at Cooper Union was talking to the class while they were taking a break—they were outside sitting on the steps in the sun and I was inside working. Just as I came out the door to join them, I heard him say with his back to me, "That King is pretty good. We're going to hear from him." That's vitamins! And if I could find somebody that I could say that to—that's what I'd like to say to them.

JAMES KIRKWOOD

It's a tough question. The best piece of advice? Let's see, it was probably, "If you really want to do something, you can do it. If you want to do it so much it hurts, you will find a way." That was one piece of advice. The other was "Do your own thing. Don't try to copy anyone." There is hardly any plot that has not been used, but it's the way *you* tell a story that will be unique. I didn't get barrels of good advice, I don't believe.

Advice to the aspiring writer. Yes, writing is difficult, but if you really want to write, if you are obsessed with telling a story or writing a poem or an article—

What is the best piece of advice you were ever given and, what piece of advice would you offer an aspiring artist/author?

then you can do it. And you should write from your own life, use everything and everyone you've encountered. I think it is also very wise to write about something you love very much or something you hate very much. The emotion may change as you get into the writing deeper but it will motivate you in the beginning. It's also best not to discuss what you want to write with many people. That dissipates the creative muse. If you talk a story or idea too much, you can kill it off. You will feel as if you'd already *written* it, you will lose your adrenaline for the project. And keep people who tend to be negative about you and your work out of your life. Let those friends in who believe in you and are supportive, get rid of pessimists. Trust your subconscious. Many days I get through work and when I read over what I've done, I am amazed that I had that idea or came up with that character or sentence or—whatever. Writing is not a logical profession. A lot of it is mystical. Trust the mystical part of it, go along with that and you will be surprised at what you come up with. Trust your talent. Also it's best, for me at least, to splash out the first draft without being overly critical. By that I mean, don't get up every day and start reading from page one. You will never finish then. Let it all come out, let it pour out and then when you've written the first draft of whatever it is, then go back and edit, rewrite, refine, etc. *GOOD LUCK!*

JOHN KNOWLES

The best piece of advice I was ever given was by Thornton Wilder, who read my work for a good ten years and was utterly invaluable as a mentor. The advice he gave me was, "In writing there should always be an element of play." That is, you don't write with your will and a driving force, that it is a kind of a form of play. Even though you are writing something dead serious, there must be an element of play in the work, your approach to the work, and even your doing of the work.

Remember it is an art form. You are not growing potatoes, you are not digging coal—you are involved in an art form. You approach it with a certain thing that you must call playfulness.

ELMORE LEONARD

Well, my advice to new writers today is just read, read, read, and find someone whom you feel you have some kind of kinship in attitude and study it. Study that particular writer—the way the writer puts it down, the way the writer paragraphs, the way the writer punctuates, everything. Which is what I did with Hemingway.

ROY LICHTENSTEIN

Watch the whole painting you are working on and muscularly sense the position of the mark you are making in relationship to your whole vision.

And that would be the same advice that I would pass on.

ROBERT LUDLUM

Read—that is terribly important. Become as well read as you can. Try to understand what is behind the writing of a given work. Then write as much as you can. Even if you've finished a book, take ten or fifteen minutes out of the day and look out the window and describe something you see and put it on a piece of paper. Because it is all a question of sharpening the tools of your trade. Think in terms of craft before you think in terms of art.

ALISON LURIE

Turn in and use your own life experience rather than try to reach out to worlds you don't know. That was right for me. There are many wonderful writers who will tell stories about times and places they've never been. For me, it was right to work closer to home.

Make time for writing. Take notes of things you see. Don't try to write about something you know nothing of.

My undergraduate students often believe that they've got to write about very dramatic events. I think it comes from watching too much television—that there

What is the best piece of advice you were ever given and, what piece of advice would you offer an aspiring artist/author?

has to be murders, there has to be violence, there has to be melodrama, there has to be exotic settings. So when they write stories with this in mind, they are not writing from their own experience, but from their experience with television or movies. So I tell them—write about what you know, what you have seen, thought, and felt.

JOHN D. MACDONALD

Show, don't tell. Don't write "He was a clumsy man." Show him falling down stairs. Don't say, "She was a difficult woman." Show her in one of her periods of hostility. Use this same approach to scenes. How does it look, smell, sound, taste, feel. The sensory image creates that illusion of reality which takes the reader *into* a book and makes him forget that he is involved in the act of reading.

I would tell the neophyte writer that if he hasn't been reading constantly all his life up to that point, forget it. Prose by writers whose reading has been limited is invariably clumsy, stilted, awkward, trite, and cliché ridden. There *must* be an intense and long-term exposure to the art form one is emulating. If not, it is like a blind man trying to paint.

Also remember that the written word—for entertainment—is but a tiny part of public attention. Today a novel which sells 60,000 copies can make the best-seller lists. As a writer you are way off in left field, with the game called on account of rain. Only 6 percent of America reads anything beyond the daily paper and what is required in the job. Thirty million adult Americans are functionally illiterate. So never, never try to please a particular audience or a particular public taste. By the time you can reach it, it is gone. Witness the current demise of the spy and intrigue novel. Write to please yourself. You are the only significant audience.

Avoid antsy-fancy writing. Delete it when you commit it. You have done it only to please your mother.

THOMAS MCGUANE

Work like a man in any other job, every day, with the weekend off.

ROLLIE MCKENNA

I would say, in answer to both questions—do what you really enjoy doing.

WILLIAM MANCHESTER

The best advice I've ever been given is the best advice I could give, and that is— never quit, never quit, *never* give in! A great disappointment can turn in to be a blessing in disguise. In 1945 when Churchill lost the prime ministry, his wife Clementine said, "This very well may be a blessing in disguise." He said, "If that's true, it's sure well disguised."

Our personal victories teach us nothing. We learn only from our defeats. It's the mistakes that we've made that teach us. I just sold a story to the *New York Times Magazine*. I learned nothing from that but, if it had been rejected, I would have been disappointed, but undoubtedly—I would have learned something. As I look back, the books that were turned down were greater learning experiences for me, as well as the books that were well reviewed, but did not sell. That's how I put together a writing career without realizing it at the time.

CONRAD MARCA-RELLI

You know that is a very difficult question because, frankly, I am pretty disappointed in what's happening to the whole art world. I find it so unpredictable that it would be hard to tell a young man what to do, unless you went back into the history of time and said, "Painting is its own reward." The artist should never forget to be an artist. Be involved in the problem of making a painting. Avoid the shortcuts of finding something too easy and too quick and too soon. It's nice that painting has problems, that it has an insolvable possibility so that you're involved

What is the best piece of advice you were ever given and, what piece of advice would you offer an aspiring artist/author?

with it all your life. That's, in fact, the beauty of art—you never solve it. Which is difficult to do today because between the media and the quick success story, and the fact that artists are supposed to get a retrospective at a museum when he is twenty-four and he's a has-been at twenty-six. This is the kind of tempo that is very bad for creative people. It doesn't give them a chance to mature. It doesn't give them a chance to seek out that form of expression which takes longer to do. Nobody has the time because they want to make it quick.

There is a human need of artists in general to feel some kind of an echo to what they are doing. They would like to have encouragement. They would like to feel that they're having a show, but the show is no longer a show where you show other painters what you're doing. In the time of the abstract expressionist early period, we were artists without an audience. Just artists went to look at other's shows—nobody else went.

JAMES MERRILL

I can't remember taking anyone's advice! Not about my work, at least. But I remain forever grateful to the people who recommended certain writers, certain books that weren't part of my "formal" education: Proust, Lady Murasaki, Elizabeth Bishop, E. F. Benson, Cavafy—to name only a few.

To an aspiring writer? Read a lot, and don't take anyone's advice about your writing.

JAMES A. MICHENER

I was not blessed with a lot of advice when I was young. I'm not sure I would have listened to it had it come my way.

My advice to young writers is to be sure that they have their first novel read by Rogers and Hammerstein, because if it can be converted into something like *South Pacific*—they are in good shape.

I think that all of the arts are interlocked and interrelated. Someone who wants to be a writer, or an architect, or a poet, or a dramatist, who is not aware of what's being done in the fellow arts—is cheating herself or himself. I think a writer needs to know what is being done in dance, and in architecture, and in city planning. Just as the city planner needs to know what is being done in the arts.

JULES OLITSKI

Go and work. Don't you realize you are going to die?

Artists use things. Using death is useful, at least I find it useful. If I say to myself, Hey you—you could drop dead any minute, you know. Come on, do something! And then it happens, then you do it. And if that doesn't do it, you do it again. Some of my paintings got very heavy from doing it over and over and over until I did something. You use whatever you can. Artists are very selfish that way.

Don't drink. Go to museums and look at the old masters (as well as the modern masters), so that you get the "smell" of great art into your very being. And look at bad art too, so that you don't forget its stench no matter how it may disguise itself as avant-garde, or whatever.

What is the best piece of advice you were ever given and, what piece of advice would you offer an aspiring artist/author?

LARRY POONS

Shut up and drink your milk.

The people that will make art or literature that *does* make a difference—they don't need advice. They're running on instinct already. The art will be made. It *will*, sooner or later, be seen for what it is. If you think you know where you're going to be (in your art) X years from now, that's where you're at now but you're just putting it off.

Great art is not something that you can learn. If you could learn it—then it could be taught and you'd have generations of great artists. So often the emphasis is on technique and that's what they try to teach in schools as being the key to great art. It's irrelevant. It'll get you a job in an ad agency as a paste-up, but it doesn't have anything to do with great art. Just like the person that you fall in love with doesn't have to be loved by everyone else, even in your immediate family. That's not important. It's only important if you love them. The same thing with art. It's not important that there's a big consensus out there that your art is great. If there is, it's probably not, because there just aren't that many people out there who really can see that well, or hear that well, or read that well. When so-called subject matter is a substitute for content, then it becomes popular art or popular music. That's what's been built up in the world for the last twenty-five to thirty years. It is not the art that I make—just like I don't write popular songs.

PADGETT POWELL

Don't redo Faulkner.

Be strong, be strong, be brave and don't quit, and don't go around telling people you're a writer.

ROBERT RAUSCHENBERG

I think the best advice was from Morris Kantor, and I can't remember what he said.

I would advise a young artist to mind his own business. The art world in America is not like it was when I was growing up. It's so successful commercially, politically, and economically that there are so many distractions. Take enough aesthetic vitamins so that you're not corrupted by the trends or the money or the galleries. It is an individual search for a kind of truth that one is after, and that truth should be unique. Every time you do a piece, you have to prove that there is only one of you in existence.

LARRY RIVERS

I don't remember.

Just keep finding things that are positive and keep yourself excited and interested, and work. There's nothing else to do. Now a lot of people don't feel that way. They feel that painting is just one more part of a whole existence. Like they do this, they do that, they've got a home, they work around the house, they work out in the garden—then they paint. I hardly do anything except paint. I do play music though.

JAMES ROSENQUIST

Do it now, but do it!

Do it now, don't wait!—because in 1950 a world-class artistic statement was made by Jackson Pollack in a small barn in East Hampton, working on the floor using a minimal of means. He probably didn't even have electricity.

*What is the best
piece of advice you
were ever given and,
what piece of advice
would you offer an
aspiring artist/author?*

BOB SHACOCHIS

When I was a freshman or sophomore in high school, my father said, "If you don't get your hair cut, you're never going to get a job with the government." That's certainly the piece of advice that changed my life. I've always reacted against advice and did the opposite thing. I was a terrible student and a terrible advice taker.

I lived in Rome and I had the opportunity to get up on the scaffolding in the Sistine Chapel. I could actually touch the ceiling and see in the fresco where Michelangelo had made mistakes. My advice would be that your failures are more important than your successes. They teach you more. They clarify your character. Surviving your mistakes has everything to do with where you go from there and it's usually a positive place.

WILFRID SHEED

My father used to put his head in his hands and groan if I made a mistake in English. I couldn't write a letter to him until I was about forty. He was a big influence simply in that he always gave books for Christmas. He gave me books that he knew I would enjoy. He gave me a book about the Algonquin which made me crave to come back to New York even more than I already did. Another book my father gave me that was really useful was *Pilgrim's Progress*, because that is a kind of English that has totally disappeared. In fact, any quotation you see from the seventeenth century has a strength to it that nobody has had since. In general, my father put me on to good prose, but I cannot remember any one thing he said.

The only thing that did me any good in school, until I discovered history, was Latin. I would definitely recommend that an aspiring writer learn Latin. The only grammar I ever learned was Latin grammar. It's the literature that you can reach. I suddenly found, with this thrill, that I was enjoying reading Virgil. I tried the same thing with Greek and certainly loved reading what I could of Sophocles particularly, but I didn't enjoy the language. First, because nobody knew what it sounded like, which was a problem. Latin gives you a great appreciation of language and sound. I was learning Latin at about the same time I was discovering poetry. The whole thing was a kind of glorious sound orgy for me.

ISAAC BASHEVIS SINGER

Write about the things you know best. Stay in your own corner of the world and do not go to a foreign country and try to write a book about it. Write about your own village, the place and the people you know. Be well and succeed with your book.

PATRICK D. SMITH

Never give up as a writer no matter what—never be defeated—have faith in yourself and what you are doing—and just keep going forward. At least *try*.

That is the same advice I would give to an aspiring writer, plus this: write from the heart.

SYD SOLOMON

Harold Rosenberg once *advised* me—he said, "Never try to give advice to young painters. Not even by example."

ROBERT STONE

I think the best advice anybody ever gave me was to make sure you know what you want, as opposed to what you think you're supposed to want.

I think that what I would tell writers now is, you can never transcend the process of storytelling. Storytelling is something that can't be transcended by intellectual content. Basically, a writer is always telling a story. The thing stands or falls on the effectiveness of the storytelling. The one thing you can't be is boring, no matter how serious you want to be—you've got to sustain the story.

What is the best piece of advice you were ever given and, what piece of advice would you offer an aspiring artist/author?

PETER TAYLOR

Don't be afraid of the dark.

Writing is making sense of one's life. It is coming to understand yourself. That is what I tell young writers and that is what I love about Katherine Anne Porter. She interpreted the events of her own life in her stories, by just writing them down.

JERRY N. UELSMANN

Most real growth involves an element of pain. It involves an element of confusion as you move to the limits of your understanding. If you are going to do anything that is fresh, you really have to force yourself to go to the limits of your own understanding. In a way, successful people probably make more mistakes because they take more chances.

RICHARD WILBUR

My wife advised me for a long time, year after year, to throw the ball higher when serving at tennis; when I finally did as she suggested, my serve improved sharply. Various people have taught me how to double-knot my shoelaces, how to swing a scythe, how to use shims in reconstructing a stone wall. Someone advised me to bend my knees when lifting a heavy sack. Robert Frost told me never to think of a good line first, and write up to it.

My advice to aspiring poets is to read widely in all periods, and if possible in several languages; also to be influenced by fifty poets at once, so as not to copy the style of any one poet.

CHARLES WILLEFORD

I would advise anybody to write about what they know—which is good advice. If he's writing about what he doesn't know that will force him to look something up. Too often, writers don't verify their information.

Publishers are all looking for the Big Book. So it's very difficult for young writers to get published. When they do get published, they don't get reviewed because there are so many blockbusters coming out with a lot of advertising behind them. On the other hand, there's a big boom in small presses and I would advise young writers to start there. The idea is to get published and build your audience. Small presses usually put out books that are a labor of love, that look good, and that look professional.

JOY WILLIAMS

I wish I could remember good advice. I never can seem to. Your work must be the most important thing in your life.

SECOND TAKES

MELBOURNE, 1986

KEY WEST, 1999

KEY WEST, 1998

KEY WEST, 1988

SARASOTA, 1983

"CAMERA AND WALL-RELIEF SERIES"

SARASOTA, 1983

GAINESVILLE, 1988

GAINESVILLE, 1988

KEY WEST, 1999

COCONUT GROVE, 1986

DAVIE, 1983

KEY WEST, 1988

CORAL GABLES, 1988

KEY WEST, 1988

NORTH PALM BEACH, 1992

ROY LICHTENSTEIN

CAPTIVA, 1987

SIESTA KEY, 1986

SIESTA KEY, 1987

KEY WEST, 1986

CORAL GABLES, 1988

ISLAMORADA, 1985

ISLAMORADA, 1985

CAPTIVA, 1987

SOUTH BEACH, 1997

ARIPEKA, 1987

TALLAHASSEE, 1993

SURFSIDE, 1998

SIESTA KEY. 1983

GAINESVILLE, 1988

KEY WEST, 1988

SOUTH MIAMI, 1988

SIESTA KEY, 1983

Having viewed the early portraits of this collection as a museum exhibition in 1989, and now having the revised and expanded version about to be presented in book form, I find myself looking back on events that helped shape my career and eventually allowed the idea of personal photographic tributes to become more than a passing impulse.

Other than my mother, who opened my world by reading stories to me and giving me books filled with words, paintings, and photographs when I was a child, and my Uncle Ed Halsey, whom I'd looked up to as a big brother and mentor— my boyhood heroes were artists and writers: the painters Franz Kline, Willem de Kooning and Robert Motherwell; authors such as Hemingway, Hart Crane and Tennessee Williams. Since art was not taught in the high school I attended half-heartedly, I turned to books outside the classroom, especially in-depth accounts of certain artists whose work I knew and followed with interest, but whose formative years and personal lives I knew little to nothing about. From Henry Miller's *Tropic of Cancer* to Arthur Rimbaud's *Illuminations* and even Irving Stone's *The Agony and the Ecstasy,* I read not only for biographical data, but for useful insight and clues to my own nature.

Through grammar school and junior high, I was given special consideration because of a natural ability to draw. When I moved up to Miss Ledeau's art classes in the higher grades, I first saw my own paintings displayed not only in the halls at school, but in the then rare light of approval in my mother's eyes. Compensating for the lack of formal art education, I found books that also told me something about the dawning of the High Renaissance in Florence; the sun-flowers of Arles and the brown-skinned girls of Tahiti; a mix of memorable characters, fighting bulls, Rioja and Fundador in Pamplona; and the gathering of post-war artists and writers on the Left Bank of the Seine.

In the midst of the eleventh grade and a conservative, buttoned-down household, I broke out with a rash of Bohemian tendencies. While my classmates were cramming for exams, sharpening their team skills, or sipping daddy's bourbon and rehearsing good ol' boy belches, I retreated into a private world of blues and jazz, abstract expressionism, and Golden Gloves boxing. Naturally, I began to write, my only audience being screen-dancing moths and the wild-eyed gecko that hung out nightly in the after-hours light of my window. Then my Uncle Ed gave me his vintage 35mm Zeiss Contaflex. I was seventeen.

This hand-me-down camera provided a new way to see and communicate. My photographs began to function like a silent, second language, allowing me to share an idea or an experience without uttering a word. Peering through the lens, I could take slow or split-second black and white compositions from different forms of local color I wanted to record—from a shadow or reflection that took on added meaning when framed in the viewfinder to my father's acceptance of a championship flight golf trophy being presented to him at the Country Club; from the algae-stained angels of a terraced nineteenth century cemetery to a dead red-tailed hawk nailed crucifixion style to a roadside barn; from my first figure studies to the porch-shaded birthplace of poet Sidney Lanier. I had found a way to freeze an observation and preserve it. My camera saw what I saw, but offered a more precise memory than the one I'd used for exams and curfews.

Nevertheless, I continued to pursue my old interest in painting. Compared with photography, painting still seemed a more natural and open-ended form of self-expression. Drawing and painting slowed me down to a point where, selecting a pencil or a brush, I could reproduce or reinvent what I saw.

In 1964, I emerged from academia with majors in Painting and Art History, a B.F.A. degree in one hand, a Zeiss Contaflex swinging from the other. Which hand to follow? Trusting instinct, I moved to Atlanta to find work in which I could expand upon my academic training. My first employer turned out to be

Jerome Drown, one of the leading advertising photographers in the Southeast. A demanding taskmaster of the old school, Drown started me out in the darkroom where, as printmaker, I enlarged his illuminating black and white negatives and rendered them onto varying sizes and surfaces of paper by painting with light. He reviewed my work more as philosopher than boss. By his example, I saw firsthand how one gifted photographer had maintained artistic integrity in the marketplace of commercial ideas and images. Grateful for over a year of apprenticeship and on the best of terms with my tutor himself, I moved on in the unlikely position of Room Manager with Playboy Clubs International. To keep the light hours free to photograph, and paint, I ran the Penthouse of the newly opened Atlanta club by night. After another year, good feelings and my early promotion aside, I faced the fact I had deluded myself. I knew all about holding rehearsals and lighting-on-cue with pastel-tinted pin spots for entertainers such as Flip Wilson, Gloria Loring, Charlie Callas, Donna Theodore, and Gregory Hines, "beverage averages" and Bunny tantrums, but what my horizons as a photographer or painter might be remained obscure.

Accepted by the Graduate School of New York University, I took off to continue my education and explore the Greenwich Village and museum galleries I'd read about in the back rows of my high school algebra class. At first, it was like waking up to a full blown surreal sequel of my schoolboy daydream—to a loud urban landscape of engaging dimensions as I discovered concentrations of the great art of the past and present within walking distance of my small mid-town apartment. I could actually stand before many of the canvases I knew only from slide shows and volumes of art history—particularly those of Cezanne, Matisse, Modigliani, Picasso, Pollock—and, of growing interest to me, portraits by Hals, Rembrandt, Sargent and Velasquez. Other than the popular exhibitions organized by Edward Steichen, and then the provocative shows curated by John Szarkowski at the Museum of Modern Art, contemporary still photography was frequently overlooked and seldom displayed by other metropolitan museums of art at the time. Regardless, I located some privately owned salons, including the

Witkin Gallery, and looked at original black and white prints by masters such as Adams, Brassai, Cartier-Bresson, Evans, Strand, and Bill Brandt, a modernist whose published folio, *Perspective of Nudes,* left an impression that stayed with me.

Then, at the time of my prearranged visit with Brandt at his flat outside London on a cold and dreary December day in 1966—whose warm hospitality, vivid recollections of his mentor Man Ray and Paris in the late-twenties, as well as a private showing of his close-ups of the eyes of the painters and sculptors Giacometti, Dubuffet, Ernst, Nevelson, and Arp, left me appreciative not only of the moment, but of the liberating effect his abstract photographic studies and unconventional compositions had had in the development of my camera and darkroom work.

One night, shortly after I had completed graduate study, I started a walk along those familiar streets of the East Side that eventually brought me back to the triple-locked door of my apartment. Somewhere on the way back to East 62nd Street and 2nd Avenue, I'd sealed a quiet pact with myself to try my hand at starting up a business. I had also reached that stage of life in the big city where its once daily magic had begun to fade. I found myself less concerned that two photographs of mine were about to be published in the U.S. Camera World Annual than the fact that I'd come to a phase of discontent. I wanted to see the return of two paintings I'd nearly completed and found missing during my final semester as a graduate student; I wanted to breathe clean air; I wanted to park my car outside my door instead of at the far end of the 59th Street Bridge; I wanted to find a downtown building with character and rent-control for my studio and residence; to start in on the design of my new business cards; to spend time with my mother and father; to get back to basics. Then, with one eye on the New York art scene, and the other on a distant, less-frenzied setting, I packed my portfolio and belongings, settled my accounts and personal affairs, and headed for Florida.

Making use of my background in painting and my progress in photography, I began to photograph people for a living. Photography had come easy, but when it became more than a part-time involvement I had to learn to balance artistic leanings with unproved business capabilities. I opened my Orlando studio in 1971. But not before taking care of the last-minute details I'd reserved until the night before I opened for business. In the final hours of May, with a sense of having the missing pieces of a puzzle at hand, I placed a fetching portrait in the display window and hung my new sign from under the white wood balcony of this quaint two-story building which, even in the faint glow of the corner street lamp, was of another time and place. An architectural anachronism that had remained, in form and function, more in concert with the narrow nineteenth century facades facing out onto Bourbon or Duval Street than with the neighboring brick and stucco storefronts lining North Orange Avenue. For me, this dated structure, ca. 1908, offered a slice of "Old Florida" as home and workplace. Out back were tall oaks, climbing vines and lizards, and canopies of exotic vegetation—the beginnings of a hidden garden with tropical settings I could use in staging a portrait, or in personal work. Upstairs was the same claw-footed tub and heart pine flooring that had helped support a tradition of "living-above-the-store" for a variety of previous shopkeeps and professionals: the small family and owner of a service station, a restaurateur, an attorney, a realtor, beautician, barber, and, as rumor had it, an enterprising entrepreneur who operated as a seamstress by day and hooker by night. Now that I'd settled in, the studio lights, backdrops, samples of work, camera and tripod, darkroom and dressing room all in place, the phone started ringing and I began to schedule my first appointments.

Subsequently I was invited to design a curriculum and teach this new series of photography classes and workshops at the nearby Loch Haven Art Center (now the Orlando Museum of Art). In the decade that followed, I was gratified to see a number of my students receiving regional and national awards, exhibition space, as well as college credit for these evening courses in which I held drawing sessions; gave lectures, weekly photo-assignments and critiques; brought in models for "nude night;" and presented photography not only as a means to develop "an eye," but a legitimate art form. Also gratifying was seeing my work appearing in magazines from the Popular Photography and the *US Camera World Annuals* to *Rolling Stone* and *Vogue;* on record album covers from *Idlewild South* by the Allman Brothers Band to *The Best of Otis Redding;* in corporate ads and political campaigns and annual reports; up on billboards; and, finally, in museum galleries.

At the time it seemed that I was on track and making progress in my new career, but I was not without a nagging awareness of having neglected my personal work in the process. Then came the unforseen events of an otherwise routine day that led to my engagement with a disturbing tirade, the content of which held the beginnings of a new perspective and agenda for me as a photographer. After securing and locking up the studio, I stepped outside the building and at once dropped my plan of a late afternoon run when I was faced by the deafening pronouncements of a looming thunderstorm. Calling it a day, I headed up the stairs, settled in and switched on channel 24. As the screen came to life I became less concerned with the rumblings outside than what was then heating up before my eyes. I watched with interest as a loud high-pitched verbal outburst changed the look on the face of talk show host Dick Cavett. His unsettled guest at that time, writer Truman Capote, had seized the moment to denounce a harsh review of Tennessee Williams's latest play as personal, and anything but a competent appraisal of the work itself (Williams's earlier works included acclaimed plays such as *The Glass Menagerie, Sweet Bird of Youth, A Streetcar Named Desire, The Night of the Iguana,* as well as poetry and prose). Capote went on to assertively point out, and I paraphrase, in Europe the artists of their time are honored and allowed to rest on their laurels. Here in America they remain under a microscope and have to keep proving themselves over and over again. Replaying this scenario over in my head, troubling as I found it to be, I dared to ask myself—what then, if anything could I do?

In 1983, I was surprised to discover how many internationally noted artists, authors, poets, and playwrights were then living and working in Florida. As an undergraduate, I had admired the collages of Conrad Marca-Relli; the abstract paintings of Syd Solomon; and the crushed car-skin sculptures of John Chamberlain. The presence on the gulf coast of each of these artists triggered the idea of a collection of photographic tributes; that, and the sudden death of Tennessee Williams, the first of the writers I had hoped to photograph and perhaps best known of them all.

In March of that same year, I photographed John Chamberlain in Sarasota. The experience of having the elusive sculptor generously give more than rehearsed expressions to my camera made me feel I'd come upon an idea whose time was long past due. Why had no one ever portrayed the artists and writers of their time who had migrated to this sub-tropic scratch-mark on the globe? The Florida seascapes of Winslow Homer were well-known. But how many knew that other late nineteenth century artists such as George Innes, Martin Johnson Heade, Thomas Moran, and John Singer Sargent had also painted in Florida? And there were the nineteenth century writers Stephen Crane, Ralph Waldo Emerson, James Whitcomb Riley, and Harriet Beecher Stowe. Other twentieth-century authors who found this outlying retreat a useful haven included Elizabeth Bishop, John Dos Passos, Robert Frost, Ernest Hemingway, James Leo Herlihy, Jack Kerouac, Marjorie Kinnan Rawlings and Wallace Stevens, not to mention the Florida born writers George Garrett, and Zora Neale Hurston. Now, there were others of note. Research revealed fourteen important American artists, a Nobel Prize Laureate, a dozen Pulitzer Prize winners, seven recipients of the National Book Award, and nine of the world's top producers of best-sellers. Given Florida's rich history of illustrious resident artists and writers, I could not believe that I was the first to focus a camera on the subject.

I continued my photographic interviews with Conrad Marca-Relli and Syd Solomon in their respective studios, on that first day in Sarasota. In the nineteen years that followed, I would photograph forty-seven others, a number of these personalities — Ann Beattie, John Malcom Brinnin, Harry Crews, Annie Dillard, James Kirkwood, Alison Lurie, John D. MacDonald, Jules Olitski, James

Rosenquist, Robert Rauschenberg, Robert Stone, and Richard Wilbur—more than once, over time, in the expansion of this collection. Famous as they were, most of my subjects were charming and without pretense, some even camera shy. I was impressed by their candor and lack of artifice—qualities I wanted to capture. I also wanted to shed light on where and how their work was done. With this perspective, I would be able to present familiar names with, often, unfamiliar faces in their own surroundings.

Was their attraction to the coastal waters of Florida in any way similar to what had drawn an earlier generation to the Left Bank of the Seine? Were they seeking solitude, subject matter, a simpler time and place, or merely seasonal ease? Historians may supply answers. What mattered most to me was the opportunity to preserve the phenomenon itself and to identify these distinguished men and women on film.

J. R.
Orlando, 2005

I want to convey particular thanks to the fifty distinguished men and women featured in this gallery of portraits. Each one generously gave of their time and graciously cooperated with my camera. For their work, as well as their participation in this project, I extend my admiration and gratitude.

For the important role that each one played in the development of this book, I owe a number of people special thanks. I am grateful to Peggy Hill who, across the years, shared the vision and selflessly helped to see it take shape. My gratitude to John D. MacDonald, not only for his introduction of the book, but his words of encouragement in the early going. This book, over twenty years in the making, has benefitted from the personal interest and wise counsel of John Malcolm Brinnin, who wrote the foreword and in whose debt I remain. I thank Phil Walden, founder of Capricorn Records, patron of the arts, and the thoughtful individual who first brought this collection to the attention of Mercer University Press. For his ongoing interest and valuable support since the time the idea of this project initially surfaced in 1983, many thanks to Don Carter. For those late nights of literary enlightenment and repartee—Eliot, Stevens, Thomas, Woolf, Pound, Shakespeare and Co., for recollections of "Fundador!" cheers and thanks to John McKinney. I am grateful to Ray Fleming for taking me to a retrospective showing of John Chamberlain's sculpture at the John and Mable Ringling Museum of Art in Sarasota, in 1983, and for the introductions and conversation with Chamberlain that took place later that night in his Tenth Street studio.

For their own contribution, knowingly or not, I would like to acknowledge the following: Heidi Anderson, Pat Armstrong, Pete Barr, Sr., Steve Boetto, Judith Ciardi, Beverly Coe, Gloria Cone, Debby Day, Joe DeGrandis, Berniece

Doughty, Buddy Ferguson, Rusty Flynn, Bradley Fray, Betsy Halloway, Ed Hayes and Betty Ann Weber, Jean Hill, Patrice Hill, Capt. Reo Hill, Sam and Angela Jacobson, Rosemary Jones, Sims Kline, Wright Langley, Dorothy Lichtenstein, Dorothy MacDonald, Kevin McCarthy, Chauncey Mabe, Mari Michener, Marj Myers, Bill Nolan, Alison Devine Nordstrom, Kim O'Brien, Kristina Olitski, Susan Olsen, Todd Persons, Doug and Pam Reagh, Tom E. Roberts, Jan Royal, Ned Sarvin, Marcus Sharpe, Walter and Jean Shine, Anne Siderius, Alma Singer, Annie Solomon, George Stuart, Jr., Jacob Stuart, Jonathan Thomas, Clark and Nancy Waters, Betsy Willeford, Capt. Charlie Wood, Lorraine Wood, and, finally, for the pleasure of their company while everyone else was asleep or away, I thank my feline friends at the time, Jackson in Orlando, Tillie in Marathon Key, and these days at "2112," Miss Havana..

For their support and assistance, I thank the State of Florida, Department of State Division of Cultural Affairs, Jim Hinson and the Dr. P. Phillips Foundation, The Seventh Annual Key West Literary Seminar, The Orlando Museum of Art, and the Research Department of the Orlando Public Library.

Publishing a book of this type requires the involvement of a number of dedicated and talented people. My appreciation to Marc Jolley and the entire staff at Mercer University Press for their interest and care in bringing this body of work out in book form.